BLACK IMAGE

BLACK IMAGE

on the AMERICAN STAGE

a bibliography
of plays
and musicals
1770-1970

by

James V. Hatch

DBS PUBLICATIONS, INC.

DRAMA BOOK SPECIALISTS

NEW YORK, NEW YORK

PREFACE

The Black man arrived on this continent when the white man arrived; indeed, one of Columbus' pilots, Alonzo Pietro, was called "il nigro." It is not surprising then to find that from the beginning, the Black image, however distorted in the recording, has been present in American history and literature.

This bibliography with its two-thousand plus entries is testimony to the continual presence of the Black image on the American stage. A perusal of these plays will reveal the growth of Black stereotypes and themes presented in ignorance and sometimes in malice by white authors. A reading of the plays listed here will reveal the attempts of Black playwrights to present some aspects of truth and reality about Negro life in America.

The last half of the decade of the 1960's has seen the rediscovery of the Black man's role in American history. Many drama teachers are now learning that plays about Nat Turner, Crispus Attucks, and Frederick Douglass were written in the 1920's and 1930's by Blacks.. Black militant plays did not wait until the 1960's; Marita Bonner published "The Purple Flower" in 1928. William Wells Brown published "The Escape; or a Leap For Freedom" in 1858.

If this bibliography will encourage teachers to explore more plays which show the development of the various Black images, if it will encourage students to examine our racial history in terms of theatre, if it will enlighten anyone about the cracked mirror which the theatre has held up to us for the last 200 years, then this bibliography will have served its purpose.

James V. Hatch
May, 1970

ACKNOWLEDGMENTS

The following men gave of their time, talents, and scholarship to help locate many plays and sources. For much that is good in this collection, these men deserve credit: Dr. Roderick Bladel, Librarian, Library and Museum of Performing Arts, New York City; Mr. Arna Bontemps, Curator, James Weldon Johnson Memorial Collection, Yale University; Mr. Steve Carter, Negro Ensemble Company, New York City; Mr. Donald Fowle, Librarian, Library and Museum of Performing Arts, New York City; Mr. James T. Maher, author and popular music historian, New York City; Mr. Whitman Mayo, New Lafayette Theatre Agency, New York City; Mr. Loften Mitchell, playwright and Black drama historian, New York City; Mr. Donald Petty, Librarian, Cohen Library, City College of New York; Dr. Thomas Pawley, Head of Humanities, Lincoln University, Jefferson City, Missouri; Dr. William R. Reardon, Drama Department, University of California at Santa Barbara; Dr. George Savage, Theatre Arts Department, University of California at Los Angeles; and Mr. Ellwoodson Williams, playwright, Manhattan Community College, New York.

CONTENTS

INTRODUCTION

CRITERIA FOR SELECTION OF ENTRIES

In most cases, a play included in this bibliography must meet two of four criteria: 1.) it contains at least one Black character; 2.) it was written by a Black playwright; 3.) it is on a Black theme; 4.) the play was written or produced in America between the years 1767 and 1970.

This bibliography includes full length plays, one acts, musicals, revues, operas, and in some cases, dance dramas. The names of composers are listed only when there was an indication that they had written either part of the book and/or the lyrics.

Plays by European, African, and Asian playwrights have been included when there was evidence that performances of their works were given in the United States, e.g., Jean Genet's **The Blacks.** In one case a Black American playwright, Victor Sejour, is included although he did all his writing in France.

In the course of the research forty-eight American and European plays with Black characters pre-dating 1800 came to my attention. Although most of these plays lie outside the scope of this work, they are listed for the reader who is curious about the early Black image in Europe. There has been no attempt to collect these plays or to say that they are representative of the Black image in Europe prior to 1800.

Thirteen plays containing Black characters have been established as having been produced in America before 1800. These have been starred (*).

Excluded from this work are radio, film, and television scripts unless they were adapted for the stage. Minstrel shows and "darkie comedies" have also been excluded.

Plays and musicals which used Black actors in neutral roles have not been included, although in some cases where a Black actor created a role in the original production, it is difficult to know if the playwright intended the role to be Black.

Although this bibliography is not definitive, every effort has been made to include all major Black American playwrights and their plays, as well as all the important plays which contain Black characters and themes.

HOW TO USE THE BIBLIOGRAPHY

Plays and playwrights in this work are entered under the following format: Author. Title of play. Genre. Date. Publisher. Library where script may be found.

EXAMPLE:

RICHARDSON, Willis. **The King's Dilemma,** (one act), 1929. In **The King's Dilemma and Other Plays for Children.** New York: Exposition Press, 1956. Schom

The dating of the plays is necessarily complex. The method used is as follows:

1.) The plays are entered alphabetically by author's last name. They are arranged by decades in which the play was first produced. Production means any production, commercial or amateur.

2.) Many plays are listed which were not produced or if they were, the first production date was not found. These are noted by the use of: (unprod.).

3.) Where (unprod.) appears and is followed by a date, this date is eithert he date of composition or of copyright.

EXAMPLE:

EDMONDS, Randolph. **Doom,** (one act), (unprod.), 1924.

4.) When no production, composition, or copyright dates were available, the play is placed in an undated category at the end of either the 19th or 20th century.

EXAMPLE:

BRANCH, William, **Experiment in Black.**

5.) When the date is uncertain or there are conflicting dates, a question mark is used.

EXAMPLE:

JACKSON, William. **Four-Eleven,** (one act), 1931(?).

6.) In cases where one author has written a number of plays in one decade, these plays are listed alphabetically by title. All co-authorships are entered separately under the last name of each author.

Plays adapted from novels or stories appear only under the adapter's name.

EXAMPLE:

AIKEN, George. **Uncle Tom's Cabin,** 1852. NYP

In instances where the original author is credited in adaptation, his name is listed also.

EXAMPLE:

WRIGHT, Richard, and Green, Paul. **Native Son,** 1941. New York: Harper & Bros., 1941. NYP

If the entry is a musical, an opera, or a one act play, it is so noted. In all other cases, the entry is assumed to be a full length dramatic script.

All plays are listed alphabetically by title in the index at the back of this book.

WHERE COPIES OF PLAYS MAY BE FOUND

Where plays are available in manuscript or typescript, they are so indicated.

EXAMPLE:

BONTEMPS, Arne, and Cullen, Countee. **St. Louis Woman,** 1946. Typescript. Schom

SF or DPS placed at the end of any entry means that in addition to the typescript, the work has also been published as an acting edition by Samuel French or Dramatists Play Service.

The BEST PLAYS series covering from 1894 to the present has been given as a script source only when no other source was found. In all cases there has been no attempt to locate the first or the best edition of any play.

The following abbreviations have been used to indicate a library where a copy of the play may be located.

NYP New York Public Library at 42nd Street and Fifth Avenue.

PAL Performing Arts Library at Lincoln Center, 111 Amsterdam Avenue. (The Research Library and the Reading Room.)

SCHOM Schomburg Collection of Negro Literature and History, 103 West 135th Street, New York City.

NEC Negro Ensemble Company, St. Mark's Place and Second Avenue, New York City. (These are typescripts sent to the Company for production consideration. The inventory was taken in November 1969.)

BP Boston Public Library, Boston, Mass.

LC Library of Congress, Washington, D.C.

YL Yale University Library, the James Weldon Johnson Memorial Collection, New Haven, Connecticut.

KT Karamu Theatre, Cleveland, Ohio. This is a production manuscript collection which Dr. Fannin Belcher, Jr. listed in his dissertation in 1945. The present state of this library was not verified.

There has been no attempt to exhaust the number of plays which may be available in any of the libraries.

Several other collections and libraries of importance are not listed; these did not respond to requests for information.

Other abbreviations listed below do not refer to libraries but to production groups; this information is not consistently included for all entries, but only where it was available.

FTP Federal Theatre Project. This means that the author was related to the Federal Theatre Project, but it may or may not mean that his play was produced by FTP.

ANT American Negro Theatre. Where ANT appears, the play was produced by this group.

FST   Free Southern Theatre, 1716 N. Miro, New Orleans, La. Where FST appears, the play was produced by this group. In many cases FST can supply a copy of the play in typescript.

APT   American Place Theatre, West 46th St., New York City. Where APT appears, the play was produced by this group.

A NOTE TO THE READER

The compiler of this work accepts responsibility for all those errors which he has perpetuated as well as those errors which he has created himself.

Further, he welcomes any correction or additional data the reader may care to send him. In the event this bibliography is reprinted, such information would be valuable.

ADDISON, Joseph. Cato, 1712. London: J. Tonson, 1713. NYP

* ANONYMOUS. Robinson Crusoe; or Harlequin Friday, (Xmas Pantomime), 1781.

* BARTON, Andrew or Forest, Thomas. The Disappointment; or, The Force of Credulity, (unprod.), 1767. Philadelphia: Francis Shallus, 1796. NYP

BEAUMONT, F., and Fletcher, J. The Knight of Malta, 1647. Cambridge: University Press, 1905-12. NYP

BEHN, Mrs. Aphra. Abdelazar; or, The Moor's Revenge, 1671. London: J. Magnes and R. Bentley, 1677. NYP

BEHN, Mrs. Aphra. The Emperor of the Moon. London: R. Holt, 1687. NYP

* BICKERSTAFFE, Isaac. The Padlock, 1769. Boston: William Spotswood, 1795. NYP

* BICKERSTAFFE, Isaac. The Romp, (comic opera) 1793. Philadelphia: M. Carey, 179?. NYP

de CERVANTES, Miguel. Los Banos de Argel. In Obras Completas, Madrid, Spain: Aguilar S.A. de Ediciones, 1965.

de CERVANTES, Miguel. El Gallardo Espanol. In Obras Completas, Madrid, Spain: Aguilar S.A. de Ediciones, 1965.

de CERVANTES, Miguel. El Trato de Argel. In Obras Completas, Madrid, Spain: Aguilar S.A. de Ediciones, 1965.

COLMAN, George. Inkle and Yarico, 1787. London: T.H. Lacey, 1787. NYP

CROWNE, John. Calisto. London: Thomas Newcomb, 1675. NYP

* CUMBERLAND, Richard. The West Indian. Boston: Apollo Press, 1794. NYP

D'AVENANT, Sir William. The Playhouse to be Let, 1663 (?). Edinburgh: William Paterson, 1883.

DRYDEN, John. Don Sebastian, 1690. London: G. Strahan, 1726. NYP

FLETCHER, J., and Beaumont, F. The Knight of Malta, 1647. Cambridge: University Press, 1905-12. NYP

HEYWOOD, Thomas. The Fair Maid of the West. London: R. Royston, 1631. NYP

* HALLAM, Lewis. Barbadoes, 1768.

* HOARE, Prince. The Prize; or 2.5.3.8, (musical farce), (One act), 1795. New York: D. Longworth, 1805. NYP

HOWARD, John. The Duke of Lerma, 1668(?). Cambridge: The University Press, 1929.

JONSON, Ben. The Masque of Blackness, 1605. London: University, Warburg Institute Journal, 1943. NYP

KOTZEBUE, August, Von. Negro Slaves. London: T. Cadell, Jr., and W. Davies, 1796. NYP

* LEACOCK, John. The Fall of British Tyranny, 1776. In Representative Plays by American Dramatists, Vol. I, Moses, Montrose, (ed.). New York: Dutton, 1918. Reprinted Blom, 1964. PAL

LEE, Nathaniel. Sophonisba, 1675. In Five Heroic Plays, Dobree, B. (ed.). London: Oxford Press, 1960. PAL

LODGE, Thomas. The Wounds of Civil War, 1594. In Old English Plays, Dodsley, Robert, (ed.), 1874-76. NYP

M'LAREN, A. Negro Slaves; or, The Blackman and the Blackbird, 1799 (?).

MARLOWE, Christopher, or by Dekker, Haughton, and Day. Lust's Dominion. In Old English Plays, Dodsley, R. (ed.). London: 1874-76. NYP

MARSTON, John. Sophonisba, 1606. In The Plays of John Marston, Vol. 2, Wood, H. Harvey (ed.). Edinburgh: Oliver & Boyd, 1934-39. NYP

MASSINGER, Philip. The Bond-man, 1623. Philadelphia: Bradford and Inskeep, 1810. NYP

2

* MUNFORD, Robert. The Candidates, (unprod.), 1770. In Dramas From
    The American Theatre, 1762-1909, Moody, R. (ed.). New York:
    World Publishing Co., 1966. NYP

* MURDOCK, J. The Politicians; or, The State of Things, 1798. LC

* MURDOCK, J. The Triumph of Love; or, Happy Reconciliation, 1795.
    Philadelphia: R. Folwell Publishers, 1795.

PEELE, George. The Battle of Alcazar, 1594. London: C.
    Whittingham and Co., 1907. NYP

PEELE, George. King Edward the First, 1593(?). London: Oxford
    University Press, 1911. NYP

REYNOLDS, Frederic. Laugh When You Can, 1798. Philadelphia:
    T.H. Palmer, 1823. NYP

* ROBINSON, J. The Yorker's Stratagem; or, Banana's Wedding.
    New York: T. and J. Swords, 1792. NYP

* ROWSON (Haswell), Susanna. Slaves in Algiers; or, A Struggle for
    Freedom, 1794. Philadelphia: Wrigley and Berriman, 1794. NYP

SHAKESPEARE, William. Love's Labours Lost, 1591. NYP

SHAKESPEARE, William. Othello, 1604. NYP

SHAKESPEARE, William. Titus Andronicus, 1592. NYP

SETTLE, Elkanah. The Empress of Morocco, 1671. London: B. Lintott, 1698.
    NYP

SOUTHERNE, Thomas. Oroonoko, 1696. London: A.and C. Corbett,
    1760. NYP

TERENCE. The Eunuch. In Collected Works, Colman, G. (ed.). London:
    Harding and Wright, 1810. NYP

THOMSON, James. The Tragedy of Sophonisba, 1730. London: A.
    Miller, 1730. NYP

de VEGA, Lope Felix. El Premio del Bien Hablar. In Obaras Escogidas,
    Vol. II, Paris: Libreria de Garnier Hermanos, 1886.

WEBSTER, John. The White Devil, 1612. In Elizabethan Plays, Hazelton,
    S. (ed.), 1933. NYP

3

BEACH, L. Jonathan Postfree; or, The Honest Yankee (musical farce),
New York: Longworth, 1807. NYP

COBB, James. Paul and Virginia (musical), 1804. New York: D.
Longworth, 1806. NYP

CUMBERLAND, Richard. The Jew of Mogadore. New York:
David Longworth, 1808. NYP

FAWCETT, John. Obi; or, Three Fingered Jack, 1801. London:
J. and H. Purkness, 1800(?). NYP

LINDSLEY, A.B. Love and Friendship; or, Yankee Notions, 1807(?).
New York: Longworth, 1809. NYP

ALLEN, Andrew Jackson (partial author?). The Battle of Lake
Champlain, 1815.

DIMOND, William. The Aethiop; or, The Child of the Desert.
New York: D. Longworth, 1813. NYP

DUNLAP, William, or Colman, George. The Africans; or, War,
Love and Duty. Philadelphia: M. Carey, 1811. NYP

PINCKNEY, M. (?). The Young Carolinians; or, Americans
in Algiers, 1818.

TAYLEURE, Clifton W. Boy Martyrs of September 12, 1814; or, Battle
of North Point, 1859. Boston: W.V. Spencer Co., 1859.

BROWN. King Shotaway, 1823.

CLINCH, Charles Powell. The Spy; or, A Tale of the Neutral Ground,
1822. Manuscript, 1822. NYP

DIMOND, William. The Lady and the Devil, (musical drama). New
York: Murden & Thomson, 1821. NYP

DUNLAP, William. A Trip to Niagara, 1828. In Dramas from the
American Theatre 1762-1909, Richard Moody (ed.), New York:
World Publishing Co., 1966. PAL

SMITH, Soloman Franklin. The Tailor in Distress, 1823.

WOODWORTH, Samuel. The Forest Rose; or, American Farmers, 1825. New York: Samuel French, 1854. NYP

ANONYMOUS. Othello Travestie, 1836.

BARNETT, Morris. Yankee Peddler; or, Old Times in Virginia, (one act), 1837 or 1841. New York: Samuel French, 1853(?). NYP

HEATH, J.E. Whigs and Democrats; or, Love of No Politics, 1839. Richmond: T.W. White, 1839. NYP

JONES, Joseph Stevens. Captain Kyd; or, The Wizard of the Sea, 1839. Boston: W.V. Spencer, 18?. NYP

JONES, Joseph S. The Liberty Tree; or, Boston Boys in '76, 1832 or 1834. Perhaps the same as The Liberty Tree; or, The Boston Tea Party, 1854.

JONES, J.S. Moll Pitcher; or, The Fortuneteller of Lynn, 1839. New York: Samuel French, 1855. NYP

RICE, Thomas D. Bone Squash Diavolo, 1835.

RICE, Thomas D. (?). Jumbo-Jum, 1838.

STEVENS, George Lionel. The Patriot; or, Union and Freedom, 1834.

ALDRIDGE, Ira (adapter). The Black Doctor, 1847. New York: DeWitt Public House, 188? NYP

ANICET-BOURGEOIS, Auguste. The Black Doctor, 1846. Translated by I.V. Bridgeman. London: T.H. Lacy (1846?). NYP

ANONYMOUS. The Captured Slave, 1815 or 1845.

ANONYMOUS. The Quadroone, 1841.

ANONYMOUS. Star of Emancipation. Boston: Emancipation Society, 1841.

BROOKS, Shirley. The Creole; or, Love's Fetters. In Dick's Standard Plays, No. 1009, London, 1847. NYP

BURTON, W.E. A Glance at Philadelphia, 1848.

JAMIESON, George. The Revolutionary Soldiers; or, The Old Seventy-Sixer, (one act), 1847. New York: Samuel French, 1863(?). NYP

JONES, J.S. The Quadroone; or, St. Michael's Day, 1841.

LITTLE, Sophia. The Branded Hand, 1845. BP

MOWATT, Mrs. Anna Cora (Ogden). Fashion, 1845. In Representative American Plays, A.H. Quinn (ed.). New York: The Century Co., 1917. NYP

SEJOUR, Victor. La Chute de Sejan, 1849.

STEELE, Silas. The Gold Bug; or, The Pirate's Treasure, 1843.

TRUMBULL, David. The Death of Captain Nathan Hale, 1842. Hartford: E. Geer, 1845. NYP

SEJOUR, Victor. Diegarias, 1844. Paris: Imprimerie de Boule etce., 1844? Schom

SEJOUR, Victor. Le Retour de Napoleon, 1841. In Nos Hommes et Notre Histoire, Desdunes, 1911.

AIKEN, George. Uncle Tom's Cabin, 1852. In Dick's Standard Plays, No. 342, New York, 1853. NYP

ANONYMOUS. Distant Relations; or, A Southerner in New York, 1859.

BATEMAN, Mrs. Sidney. Self, 1856. In Representative Plays by American Dramatists, Moses, Montrose, (ed.). New York: Dutton, 1918. Reprinted, Blom, 1964. PAL

BOUCICAULT, Dion. The Octoroon, 1859. In Representative American Plays, A.H. Quinn (ed.). New York: The Century Co., 1917. NYP

BROUGHAM, John. Dred; or, The Dismal Swamp, 1856. New York: Samuel French, 1856. NYP

BROUGHAM, John. Life in New York; or, Tom and Jerry on a Visit, 1856. New York: Samuel French, 1856. NYP

BROWN, William Wells. Escape; or, A Leap For Freedom, 1858. New York: Samuel French, 1858. NYP

BURNETT, J.G. and Lippard, G. Blanche of Brandywine, 1858. New York: Samuel French, 1858. NYP

CONWAY, H.J. Dick, the Newsboy; or, Young America, 1853.

CONWAY, H.J. Dred; A Tale of the Great Dismal Swamp, 1856
    New York: J.W. Amerman, 1856. NYP

CONWAY, H.J. New York Patriots; or, The Battle of Saratoga, 1856.

CONWAY, H.J. Our Jeminy; or, Connecticut Courtship, (one act),
    1853. New York: Samuel French, 189? NYP

CONWAY, H.J. Uncle Pat's Cabin, 1853.

DIBDIN, Thomas. The Banks of the Hudson. In Dick's Standard Plays,
    185? NYP

JOHNSON, Samuel D. The Fireman, 1849. Boston: W.V. Spencer,
    1856. NYP

JONES, Major. Major Jones' Courtship, 1851.

JONES, Robert. The Hidden Hand, 1859. Boston: W.H. Baker, 1889.
    NYP

LEMAN, Mark, and Taylor, Tom. Slave Life; or, Uncle Tom's Cabin,
    1852. London: Webster and Co., 1852(?). NYP

LIPPARD, G. and Burnett, J.G. Blanche of Brandywine, 1858. New
    York: Samuel French, 1858. NYP

ORTON, James. Arnold. In Magazine of History, 1854.

PILGRIM, James. Garibaldi; or, The Invasion of Sardinia, 1859.

PILGRIM, James. Harry Burnham; or, The Young Continental, 1851.

PILGRIM, James. Ireland and America; or, Scenes in Both, 1852.
    New York: Samuel French, 187? NYP

PILGRIM, James. Paddy, the Piper, (one act), 1850. Manuscript. PAL

PILGRIM, James. Servants by Legacy, 1851.

POOLE, John. The Doom of Deville; or, The Maiden's Vow, 1859.

POOLE, John. Our Mess; or, The Pirate Hunters of the Gulf, 1859.

POOLE, John. War Eagle; or, The Pride of the Delaware, 1859.

PREUSS, Henry Clay. Fashions and Follies of Washington Life.
    Washington, 1857. NYP

RICE, Thomas D. Otello, (burlesque), 1853. Manuscript. PAL

SEJOUR, Victor. Andre Girard, 1858. Paris: M. Levy Freres,
    1858. NYP

SEJOUR, Victor. L'Argent du Diable, 1854. Paris: M. Levy Freres,
    1854. NYP

SEJOUR, Victor. Le Fils de la Nuit, 1856. Paris: M. Levy Freres,
    1856. NYP

SEJOUR, Victor. Les Grands Vassaux, 1859. Paris: M. Levy Freres,
    1859. Schom

SEJOUR, Victor. Le Martyr Du Coeur, 1858. Paris: M. Levy Freres,
    1858. NYP

SEJOUR, Victor. Les Noces Venitiennes, 1855. Paris: M. Levy Freres,
    1855. Schom

SEJOUR, Victor. Le Paletot Brun, (one act), 1858. Paris: M. Levy
    Freres, 1859. Schom

SEJOUR, Victor. Richard III, 1852. Paris: D. Giraud et J. Dagneau,
    1852. NYP

SEJOUR, Victor. La Tireuse de Cartes, 1850. Paris: M. Levy Freres,
    1860. NYP

SEYMOUR, Harry. Aunt Dinah's Pledge, 1853. New York:
    Dick and Fitzgerald, 185? NYP

SPERRY, Austin. Extremes, 1850.

STEELE, Silas. Our Eastern Shore Cousin!, 1859.

SWAYZE, Kate L. Ossawattomie Brown, 1859. New York: Samuel
    French, 1859(?).

TAYLEURE, C.W. Horse Shoe Robinson; or, The Battle of King's
    Mountain, 1856. New York: Samuel French, 1857(?). NYP

TAYLOR, Charles W. Dred, 1856.

TAYLOR, Charles W. Little Katy, The Hot Corn Girl, 1853.

TAYLOR, Charles W. Life in Alabama, 1850.

TAYLOR, Tom, and Leman, Mark. Slave Life; or, Uncle Tom's Cabin, 1852. London: Webster and Co., 1852(?). NYP

THOMPSON, William Tappin. Major Jones' Courtship; or, Adventures of a Christmas Eve, 1850.

TROWBRIDGE, John T. Neighbor Jackwood, 1857. Boston: Philips, Sampson, and Co., 1857. NYP

WATKINS, Harvey. The Pioneer Patriot; or, The Maid of The War Path, 1858.

WHITNEY, Daniel S. Warren: A Tragedy, 1850.

ANONYMOUS. The Southern Rebellion by Sea and Land, 1861.

BARRIERE, Theodore, and Sejour, Victor. Les Enfants de la Louvre, 1865. Paris: Michel Levy Freres, 1865. NYP

BOUCICAULT, Dion. After Dark (London by Night), 1868. London: 1868. NYP

BYRON, Henry James. Robinson Crusoe; or, Harlequin Friday and the King of the Caribee Islands, 1860. New York: Samuel French, 18? NYP

DALY, Augustin. A Legend of Norwood; or, Village Life in New England, 1867. (Private Printing), 1867.

DALY, Augustin. Under the Gaslight, 1867. New York: W.C. Wemyss, 1867. NYP

GOODRICH, Frank B. Flirtation and What Comes of It, 1860. New York: Rudd & Carleton, 1861. NYP

JAMIESON, George. The Old Plantation; or, The Real Uncle Tom, 1860.

JONES, Robert. Patriot's Dream; or, The Past, The Present, and The Future, 1861.

KELSO, J. Ringold, 1865.

MACCABE, James D. Jr. The Guerillas, 1862. Richmond: West and Johnson, 1863.

PUTNAM, Mary. Tragedy of Errors. Boston: Ticknor and Fields, 1862. NYP

ROBINSON, Solon. The Rifle. New York, 1867.

SCHONBERG, James. Oscar the Halfblood. In Dick's Standard Plays, No. 474, New York, 1867.

SEJOUR, Victor. Les Aventuriers, 1860. Paris: M. Levy Freres, 1863. NYP

SEJOUR, Victor. Compere Guillery, 1860.

SEJOUR, Victor. Les Fils de Charles Quint, 1864. Paris: Michel Levy Freres, 1865. NYP

SEJOUR, Victor. La Madone des Roses, 1868. Paris: M. Levy Freres, 1869. Schom

SEJOUR, Victor. Le Marquis Caporal, 1864. Paris: M. Levy Freres, 1865. Schom

SEJOUR, Victor. Les Massacres de la Syrie, 1860. Paris: J. Barbe, 1860(?).

SEJOUR, Victor. Les Mysteres du Temple, 1862. Paris: Colman Levy, 18? Schom

SEJOUR, Victor. Les Volontaires de 1814, 1862. Paris: M. Levy Freres, 1862. Schom

SEJOUR, Victor, and Barriere, Theodore. Les Enfants de la Louvre, 1865. Paris: Michel Levy Freres, 1865. NYP

WIGAN, Horace. A Southerner Just Arrived, (one act), 1862. London: Lacy's Acting Edition, 18? NYP

ANONYMOUS. The Tyrant! The Slave!! The Victim!!! The Tar!!!! London: T.H. Lacy, 187? NYP

BOUCICAULT, Dion. Belle Lamar, 1874. In Plays for the College Theatre, G.H. Leverton (ed.), New York: Samuel French, 1932. NYP

BRADFORD, Joseph. Out of Bondage, 1878. Manuscript. LC

BRADFORD, Joseph B. In and Out of Bondage, 1877.

BROUGHAM, John. Minnie's Luck; or, Ups and Downs of City Life, 1870.

CAMPBELL, Bartley. Fairfax; or Life in the Sunny South, 1879.
In America's Lost Plays, Vol. XIX. Princeton, N.J.:
Princeton University Press, 1941. NYP

COOKE, S.N. Out in the Street, 1875. New York: Happy Hours
Co., 187? NYP

CUMMINGS, Minnie. Suspected, 1879.

DALY, Augustin. Divorce, 1871. Manuscript. PAL

DALY, Augustin. Horizon, 1871. In American Plays, A.G. Hallins
(ed.). New York: 1935. NYP

DINSMORE, George. Col. Mulberry Sellers (The Gilded Age), 1873.

DUGANNE, A.J.H. Woman's Vows and Mason's Oaths. Chicago:
The Dramatic Publishing Co., 1874. NYP

EDWARDS, W.L. Wilfred Blakely. 1879(?).

GRIFFIN, T.J. Nat Turner; or, American Slavery, 1872.

GROVER, Leonard. Our Boarding House, 1876.

HARRIGAN, Edward. The Doyle Brothers, 1876.

HARRIGAN, Edward. The Mulligan Guard Ball, 1879. Manuscript
42b. NYP

HARRIGAN, Edward. The Mulligan Guard Christmas, 1879.
Manuscript. NYP

HARRIGAN, Edward. The Mulligan Guard Chowder, 1879.
Manuscript. NYP

HARRIGAN, Edward. The Mulligan Guard Picnic, 1878.
Manuscript 44a. NYP

HOWARD, Bronson. Moorcroft; or, The Double Wedding, 1874.

HOWARD, Bronson. Saratoga; or, Pistols for Seven, 1870.
New York: Samuel French, 1874(?). NYP

HOWELLS, William Dean. The Parlor Car, (unprod.), 1876.
Boston: Houghton, Mifflin & Co., 1883.

KIRKPATRICK, Judson. Allatoona, 1875/7.

MCCLOSKEY, J.J. Across the Continent, 1870. In Drama from
the American Theatre 1762-1909, Richard Moody (ed.). New
York: World Publishing Co., 1966. NYP

MCCLOSKEY, J.J. Pomp; or, Way Down South, 1871.

MALGUM, A. or Smith, Sam. The Blue and the Gray. Manuscript,
1873. PAL

MEADER, Fred G. Kit Carson, 1874.

MERIWETHER, Elizabeth (Avery). Ku Klux Klan; or, The Carpet
Bagger in New Orleans, Memphis, Tennessee: South
Baptist Publishing Co., 1877. NYP

MUNSON, George. An Unwelcome Return, 1877. Clyde, Ohio:
A.D. Ames, 1878. NYP

PIERRA, Adolfo. The Cuban Patriots. Philadelphia: 1873. NYP

RENAULD, John B. Our Heroes, 1873. Chicago: Dramatic Publishing
Co., 1873. NYP

ROGE, Adolph. The Golden Calf, 1879.

ROWE, George. Fifth Avenue, 1877.

ROWE, George. Wolfert's Roost, 1879.

THOMPSON, John. Dixie, Our Coloured Brother, 1873.

VAUTROT, George. At Last, 1878.

VEGIARD, J.T. The Dutch Recruit; or, The Blue and the Gray.
Clyde, Ohio: 1879.

BABCOCK, Charles W. Adrift, 1881. Clyde, Ohio: A.D. Ames, 1880.
NYP

BAKER, George M. The Flowing Bowl. Boston: Walter Baker, 1885.

BARNES, Elliot. The Blue and the Gray, 1885.

BELASCO, David. May Blossom, 1884. New York: Samuel French,
1883. NYP

BELOT, Adolphe. Black Venus, 1881.

BUXTON, Ida M. Tit for Tat, (one act). Clyde, Ohio: A.D. Ames, 1884. NYP

CAGAURAM, A.R. The Fatal Letter, 1884.

CAMPBELL, Bartley. A Brave Man, 1882(?). Manuscript. PAL

CAMPBELL, Bartley. The White Slave, 1882. In America's Lost Plays, Vol. XIX. Bloomington: Indiana University Press, 1965. PAL

DALY, Augustin. The Passing Regiment, 1881.

DAZEY, C.T. For A Brother's Life, 1885.

ELWYN, Lizzie May. Millie the Quadroon; or, Out of Bondage. Clyde, Ohio: 1888.

GILLETTE, William. Held By The Enemy, 1886. New York: Samuel French, 1898. NYP

GRAHAM, Hamilton. Lost Cause. Selma, Ala.: 1888.

GUNTER, A.C. Courage, 1883.

HARRIGAN, Edward. Cordelia's Aspirations, 1883.

HARRIGAN, Edward. Dan's Tribulations, 1884. Manuscript 86. NYP

HARRIGAN, Edward. The Major, 1881. Manuscript 38b. NYP

HARRIGAN, Edward. The Muddy Day, 1883.

HARRIGAN, Edward. The Mulligan Guard Nominee, 1880. Manuscript 43a. NYP

HARRIGAN, Edward. The Mulligan Guard Silver Wedding, 1881.

HARRIGAN, Edward. The Mulligan Guard Surprise (Party), 1880. Manuscript 46a. NYP

HARRIGAN, Edward. Pete, 1887. Manuscript. NYP

HOLLENBECK, B.W. Zion. Clyde, Ohio: A.D. Ames Publisher, 1886. NYP

HOWARD, Bronson. Shenandoah, 1888. New York: Samuel French, 1897. NYP

HOWELLS, William Dean. The Sleeping Car; A Farce. Boston: Ticknor & Co., 1883. NYP

JOHNSON, Annie L. and Tyndale, Hilgarde. In Ole Virginny.
   Typescript, 1889. LC

JONES, Robert. White Terror, 1882.

MACKAYE, Steele. A Fool's Errand, 1881.

MARBLE, Edward. Spot Cash, 1884.

MILLER, Joaquin. Forty-Nine, 1881. San Francisco: The California
   Publishing Co., 1882. NYP

MINOR, George N. Eph; or, The Slave's Devotion. Manuscript, 1888.
   LC

ROSENFELD, Sidney. A Pair of Shoes, (one act). New York:
   1882. NYP

SAMPSON, J.P. The Disappointed Bride; or, Love at First Sight,
   1883.

SAYRE, T.H. The Blue and the Gray. Typescript, 1880. LC

STEDMAN, W. Elsworth. The Confederate Spy. New York:
   T.H. French, 1887. NYP

SWARTZ, Edward. J. The Kaffir Diamond, 1888.

TILLOTSON, J.K. The Planter's Wife, 1880.

TILLOTSON, J.K. Lynwood. Typescript, 1884. LC

TOWNSEND, Charles. Uncle Tom's Cabin. New York: Wehman
   Bros., 1889. NYP

TYNDALE, Hilgarde, and Johnson, Annie L. In Ole Virginny.
   Typescript, 1889. LC

ARNOLD, James O. Uncle Tom's Freedom. Dayton, Ohio: 1893.

ALFRIEND, Edward, and Pitou, Augustus. Across the Potomac, 1899.

BELASCO, David. The Heart of Maryland, 1895. Typescript. PAL

BRADFORD, J.B. Between the Lines. Raynham, Mass.: 1894.
   Manuscript. LC

14

BROWN, J.S. A Southern Rose. Clyde, Ohio: Ames' Publishing Co., 1899. NYP

CALLAHAN, C.E. Coon Hollow, 1894.

CAMPBELL, Frank. Gettysburg, 1898.

CHASE, George B. Penn Hapgood; or, The Yankee Schoolmaster. Clyde, Ohio: Ames' Publishing Co., 1890. NYP

COLE, Bob, and Johnson, William. A Trip to Coontown, (musical), 1898-99.

CONQUEST and Pillet. The Law of the Land, 1896.

COOK, Marion and Dunbar, Paul. Clorindy; or, The Origin of the Cake Walk, (musical), 1898.

COOK, Sherwin. A Valet's Mistake. Clyde, Ohio: Ames' Publishing Co., 1894. NYP

DAZEY, Charles T. In Old Kentucky, 1893. Typescript. PAL

DETIRCHSTEIN and Valentine. A Southern Romance, 1897.

DOWNING, Laura. Defending the Flag; or, The Message Boy. Clyde, Ohio: Ames' Publishing Co., 1894. NYP

DUDLEY, S.H. The Smart Set, (musical), 1896.

DUNBAR, Paul and Cook, Marion. Clorindy; or, The Origin of the Cake Walk, (musical), 1898.

EASTON, William Edgar. Dessalines, A Dramatic Tale; A Single Chapter From Haiti's History, 1893. Galveston, Texas: J.W. Burson, Co., 1893. NYP

EATMAN, G.H. Railroad Porter's Eleven Days Round Trip. Typescript, 1898. LC

FIELD, A.J. Darkest America, (musical), 1897.

FIELDS, Louisa May. Twelve Years a Slave. Indianapolis, 1897. Typescript. LC

FISKE, Minnie Maddern. The Rose, 1893.

FITCH, Clyde. Barbara Freitchie, 1899. New York: Z. and L. Rosenfield, 1899. NYP

FOOTE, William. Evolution of Negro Minstrelsy. Typescript, 1890. LC

FYLES, Franklin. Cumberland, '61, 1897. Typescript. PAL

FYLES, Franklin. Governor of Kentucky, 1896.

GARDINER, Charles. Way Down South. Norwalk, Conn.: 1898. Typescript. LC

GIBBS, Bertha V. A Planter's Son. Typescript, 1895. LC

GILLETTE, William. Secret Service, 1895. New York: Z. and L. Rosenfield, 1896. NYP

GOODWIN, Cheever. Evangeline, (musical-burlesque), 1896.

GREENE, Clay, and Grismer, J.R. The New South, 1893. LC

GRISMER, J.R., and Greene, Clay. The New South, 1893. LC

GROENVELT, Sara B. Otille the Octoroon. Typescript, 1893. LC

GUNTER, Archibald. A Florida Enchantment, 1896.

GURNEY, E.H. The King of Coontown. Typescript, 1899. LC

HAGARTY, W.H. The Gold Bug. Chicago: 1896. Manuscript. PAL

HARRIGAN, Edward. Marty Malone, 1896.

HARRIGAN, Edward. Reilly and the Four Hundred, 1890. Manuscript 56a. NYP

HAZARD, Eleanor and Elizabeth. An Old Plantation Night. New York: Dick and Fitzgerald, 1890. NYP

HELLER, Robley. Appomattox. Abingdon, Illinois: 1899. PAL

HERNE, James A. The Reverend Griffith Davenport, 1899. In America's Lost Plays, Vol. VII – Act IV only. Princeton, N.J.: Princeton University Press, 1941. PAL

HORNE, Mary B. Plantation Bitters. Boston, 1892.

HOYT, Charles H. A Texas Steer; or, Money Makes The Mare Go!,
1890. Typescript. PAL

HUGGINS, David. At Piney Ridge, 1897. Typescript. PAL

ISHAM, John. Octoroons, (musical), 1895.

ISHAM, John W., (producer). Oriental America, (musical), 1896.

JACK, Sam T. The Creole Show, (musical), 1890.

JOHNSON, William, and Cole, Bob. A Trip to Coontown,
(musical), 1898-99.

MCCLAIN, Billy. Before and After the War, 1894. Typescript. PAL

MCCONNELL, E.W. The Old Plantation. Typescript, 1897. LC

MACDONOUGH, Glen. The Gold Bug, (farce with music), 1896.

MARBLE, Scott. Down in Dixie, 1897(?). Typescript. 1894. PAL

MARTELL & Whallen. The South Before the War, 1893.

MAWSON, H.P. A Fair Revel, 1891.

MAYO, Frank. Pudd'nhead Wilson, 1895. Typescript. PAL

MERRIMAN, Effie. Diamonds and Hearts. Chicago: The Dramatic
Publishing Co., 1897. NYP

MYLES, George B. The Winning Hand. Clyde, Ohio: Ames'
Publishing Co., 1895. NYP

ORNE, Martha Russell. Timothy Delano's Courtship. New York:
Wehman Bros., 1892. NYP

PILLET and Conquest. The Law of the Land, 1896.

PITOU, Augustus, and Alfriend, Edward. Across the Potomac, 1899.

PRESBREY, E.W. Virginia Courtship, 1898.

PURNELL, John. Swamps of Louisiana. Typescript, 1897. LC

REID, Opie. The Kentucky Colonel, 1892.

17

SALESBURY, Nate. Black America, (musical), 1895.

SANFORD, Amelia. The Ghost of an Idea. Philadelphia: The Penn Publishing Co., 1898. NYP

SEAMAN, Abel (pseud. of Frank Chase). In the Trenches. Boston: W.H. Baker, 1898. NYP

SHERMAN, John W. Virginia. Lynchburg, 1892.

SHIPP, J.A. Senegamian Carnival, (musical), 1898.

SMITH, F. Hopkinson, and Thomas, Augustus. Col. Carter of Catersville, 1892. Chicago: M.A. Donohue & Co., 1891. NYP

SMITH, Margaret. Captain Hearne, U.S.A., 1893.

STEDMAN, W.Elsworth. The Confidential Clerk, 1892. New York: T.H. French, 1892. NYP

STEDMAN, W. Elsworth. The Midnight Charge. New York: T.H. French, 1892. NYP

STEPHENS, Robert N. Down on the Suwanee River. Typescript, 1895. LC

THOMAS, Augustus. Alabama, 1891. Typescript. PAL

THOMAS, Augustus, and Smith, F. Hopkinson. Col. Carter of Cartersville, 1892. Chicago: M.A. Donohue & Co., 1891. NYP

THOMAS, Augustus. In Mizzoura, 1893. In Representative Plays by American Dramatists, 1856-1911, Moses, Montrose (ed.). New York: E.P. Dutton, 1921. PAL

TILLOTSON, J.K. Report for Duty, 1899.

TOWNSEND, Charles. Down in Dixie. Chicago, Ill: 1894.

TOWNSEND, Charles. The Spy of Gettysburg, 1891. Boston: W.H. Baker, 1891. NYP

TOWNSEND, Charles. Uncle Josh. Chicago: T.S. Denison, 1891. NYP

VALENTINE and Detrichstein. A Southern Romance, 1897.

VON HARTMAN, E. Modern Africa; or, The Triumph of Love. New York: 1893. Typescript. LC

WALKER, George, and Williams, Bert, et. al. Sons of Ham, (musical), 1899.

WHALLEN & Martell. The South Before the War, 1893.

WHYTAL, Russ. For Fair Virginia, 1895.

WILLIAMS, Bert, and Walker, George, et.al. Sons of Ham, (musical), 1899.

1800's UNDATED

ANONYMOUS. The Slave Child; or, Little Alabama. Typescript. PAL

BROWN, William Wells. Experience; or, How to Give a Northern Man a Backbone, (unprod.).

HAINES, J.T. Life of a Woman. Promptbook, (London, 18?). PAL

HAINES, J.T. My Poll and My Partner Joe. In Hiss the Villain, Booth, Michael, (ed.). New York: 1964. NYP

HARRIGAN, Edward. Barney Brogan. Manuscript 4a. NYP

SEJOUR, Victor. Cromwell. Manuscript.

SEJOUR, Victor. The Outlaw of the Adriatic; or, The Female Spy and the Chief of the Ten. London: T.H. Lacy, 18? NYP

SEJOUR, Victor. Le Vampire. Manuscript.

SWAYZE, Kate L. Nigger Sweethearts. Kansas State Historical Society, Manuscript.

ALLEN, Oscar L. My Old Southern Home. Los Angeles, Cal.: 1900.

BRADFIELD, S.G. The Old Virginia Hermit. Clyde, Ohio: Ames'
Publishing Co., 1902. NYP

BROADHURST, George, and Dazey, C.T. The American Lord, 1906.
Typescript. PAL

BROADHURST, George. Wild-Fire, 1908. In Best Plays of 1899-1909,
Mantle, Burns. PAL

BROWNE, Alice, and Gault, W. Mr. Butte from Montana. Clyde,
Ohio: Ames' Publishing Co., 1903. NYP

CARPENTER, Edward Childs. The Barber of New Orleans, 1909. In
Best Plays of 1899-1909, Mantle, Burns. PAL

CHURCHILL, Winston. Crisis, 1902. New York: Samuel French, 1927.
PAL

COLE, Bob, and MacDonough, Glen. Belle of Bridgeport, (musical),
1900.

COLE, Bob, and McNally, John J. Humpty Dumpty, (musical), 1904.

COLE, Bob and Johnson, J.W., and McNally, John. In Newport,
(musical), 1904.

COLE, Bob, and Johnson, Rosamond. The Red Moon, (musical),
1909.

COLE, Bob, and Johnson, James W. The Shoo-Fly Regiment, (musical),
1907.

COOK, Marion, and Dunbar, Paul L. Jes' Lak White Folks, (musical),
1900.

COOK, Marion, and Shipp, J.A. The Policy Players, (musical),
1900.

COTTER, Joseph. Caleb, The Degenerate: A Study in Types, Customs,
and Needs of the American Negro. Louisville: Bradley and
Gilbert, 1903. Schom

COTTRELL, Harry D. A Southern Vendetta, (unprod.?), 1906.

DAZEY, Charles T., and Broadhurst, G.H. The American Lord,
1906. Typescript. PAL

DEMILLE, Wm. C. The Warrens of Virginia, 1907. Typescript. PAL

DIXON, Rev. Thomas. The Clansman, 1906. In Best Plays of 1899-
1909, Mantle, Burns. PAL

DONNELLY, Grattan H. Carolina, 1906. Typescript. PAL

DUNBAR, Paul, and Rogers, Alex, and Shipp, J.A. In Dahomey,
(musical), 1902.

DUNBAR, Paul L. and Cook, Marion. Jes' Lak White Folks,
(musical), 1900.

DUNBAR, Paul L. Uncle Ehp's Christmas, (one act musical), 1900.

DUNN, Allen. A Country Coon. Typescript, 1900. LC

FISHER, A.L., and Zerr, J.H. Black Dick; or, The Brand of Cain.
Clyde, Ohio: Ames' Publishing Co., 1902. NYP

FREEMAN, Harry L. The Tryst, (unprod.?), 1909.

GAULT, W. and Browne, Alice. Mr. Butte from Montana. Clyde,
Ohio: Ames' Publishing Co., 1903. NYP

GRANT, Richard, and Mercer, Will. The Southerners, (musical), 1904.

GUPTILL, Elizabeth. The Little Heroine of the Revolution. Lebanon,
Ohio: March Brothers, 1906. NYP

HALLBACK, William. A Hot Coon from Mississippi. Jackson, Miss:
1902. NYP

HARRIGAN, Edward. Under Cover, 1903.

HOBART, George, et.al. Sally of Our Alley, (musical), 1902. In
Best Plays of 1899-1909, Mantle, Burns. PAL

HOBART, George, and MacDonough, Glen. The New Yorkers, (musical),
1901. In Best Plays of 1899-1909, Mantle, Burns. PAL

HOGAN, Ernest. Rufus Rastus, (musical), 1905.

JOHNSON, J.W. and Cole, Bob, and McNally, John. In Newport, (musical), 1904.

JOHNSON, James W. and Cole, Bob. The Shoo-Fly Regiment, (musical), 1907.

JOHNSON, Rosamond, and Cole, Bob. The Red Moon, (musical), 1909.

KESTER, Paul, and Middleton, George. The Cavalier, 1902. In Best Plays of 1899-1909, Mantle, Burns. PAL

LYLES, Aubrey, and Reid, Hal, and Miller, Flournoy. The Oyster Man, (musical), 1907.

MACDONOUGH, Glen, and Cole, Bob. Belle of Bridgeport, (musical), 1900.

MACDONOUGH, Glen, and Hobart, George. The New Yorkers, (musical), 1901. In Best Plays of 1899-1909, Mantle, Burns. PAL

MCNALLY, John J., and Cole, Bob. Humpty Dumpty, (musical), 1904.

MCNALLY, John L. and Cole, Bob, and Johnson, J.W. In Newport, (musical), 1904.

MERCER, Will, and Grant, Richard. The Southerners, (musical), 1904.

MIDDLETON, George, and Kester, Paul. The Cavalier, 1902. In Best Plays of 1899-1909, Mantle, Burns. PAL

MILLER, Flournoy, and Lyles, Aubrey, and Reid, Hal. The Oyster Man, (musical), 1907.

MOODY, William V. The Faith Healer, 1909. Boston: Houghton Mifflin Co., 1909. NYP

PARKER, Lottie. Under Southern Skies, 1901. Typescript. PAL

PEACOCKE, Capt. Leslie. Injustice, (unprod.?), 1906.

REID, Hal. At the Old Cross Roads, (unprod.?), 1902.

REID, Hal. The Avenger, (unprod.?), 1907.

REID, Hal, and Miller, Flournoy, and Lyles, Aubrey. The Oyster Man, (musical), 1907.

ROGERS, Alex, and Shipp, J.A. Abyssinia, (musical), 1906.

ROGERS, Alex, and Shipp, J.A. Bandanna Land, (musical), 1908.

ROGERS, Alex, and Shipp, J.A., and Dunbar, Paul. In Dahomey, (musical), 1902.

ROGERS, Alex, and Shipp, J.A., and Williams, Bert. Mr. Lode of Koal, (musical), 1909.

RYAN, Samuel. O'Day, The Alderman. Boston: W.H. Baker & Co., 1901. NYP

SHELDON, Edward. The Nigger, 1909. New York: Macmillan, 1910. Schom

SHIPP, J.A. and Rogers, Alex. Abyssinia, (musical), 1906.

SHIPP, J.A. and Rogers, Alex. Bandanna Land, (musical), 1908.

SHIPP, J.A. and Dunbar, Paul, and Rogers, Alex. In Dahomey, (musical), 1902.

SHIPP, J.A. and Williams, Bert, and Rogers, Alex. Mr. Lode of Koal, (musical), 1909.

SHIPP, J.A. and Cook, Marion. The Policy Players, (musical), 1900.

SUTHERLAND, Evelyn G. Po' White Trash, (one act). In Collected Works. Chicago: H.S. Stone, 1900. NYP

SHIPMAN, Louis E. On Parole, 1907. New York: MacMillan Co., 1923. NYP

STEPHENS, Robert N. and Swete, E. Lyall. Miss Elizabeth's Prisoner, 1908. Typescript. PAL

SWETE, E. Lyall, and Stephens, Robert N. Miss Elizabeth's Prisoner, 1908. Typescript. PAL

THOMAS, Augustus. Witching Hour, 1907. New York: Harper & Bros., 1908. NYP

WALTER, Eugene. The Easiest Way, 1909. In Representative Plays by American Dramatists, Moses, Montrose (ed.). New York: Dutton, 1918. Reprinted, Blom, 1964. NYP

WILLIAMS, Bert, and Shipp, J.A., and Rogers, Alex. Mr. Lode of Koal, (musical), 1909.

1910 - 1919

ANONYMOUS. Come Along Mandy, (unprod.?), 1917.

BABCOCK, Mrs. Bernie (Snade). Mammy. New York: The Neale Publishing Co., 1915. NYP

BOLTON, Guy, and Carleton, Tom. Children, (one act), 1916.

BOYD, E.H. Mammy, (unprod.?), 1913.

BROWN, Annie K. Voice on Wire. In Counselor Print, (1919).

BURRILL, Mary. Aftermath, (one act). (unprod.) 1919.

BURRILL, Mary. They That Sit in Darkness, (one act). In Birth Control Review, Vol. III, No. 9, (September, 1919). NYP

BYERS, Alex. Hidden Hand. Typescript, 1912. PAL

CONNOLLY, M. and Parenteau, Z. Amber Empress, (operatic comedy), 1916. In Best Plays of 1909-19, Mantle, Burns. PAL

COTTER, Joseph S. Paradox. In Saturday Evening Quill, Boston: (June, 1913).

CREAMER, Henry, and Rogers, Alexander. The Old Man's Boy, (musical), 1914.

CREAMER, Henry, and Rogers, Alex. The Traitor, (musical), 1912.

CROTHERS, Rachel. A Little Journey, (one act), 1918. New York: Samuel French, 1918.

CULBERTSON, Ernest. Rackey, (one act), 1919. In Plays of Negro Life, Locke, A. and Gregory, Montgomery (eds.). New York: Harper & Bros., 1927.

DE CAPPET, T.B. Mammy; or, The Pendeltons of Virginia, (unprod.?), 1913.

DOWNING, Henry F. The Arabian Lovers; or, The Sacred Jar. London: F. Griffiths, 1913. NYP

DOWNING, Henry F. Human Nature; or, The Traduced Wife. London: F. Griffiths, 1913. Schom

DOWNING, Henry F. Incentive, 1914.

DOWNING, Henry F. Lord Eldred's Other Daughter. London: F. Griffiths, 1913. NYP

DOWNING, Henry F. A New Coon in Town, 1914. Schom

DOWNING, Henry F. Placing Paul's Play. London: F. Griffiths, 1913. NYP

DOWNING, Henry F. The Shuttlecock; or, Israel in Russia. London: F. Griffiths, 1913. NYP

DOWNING, Henry F. Voodoo. London: F. Griffiths, 1914. NYP

DRINKWATER, John. Abraham Lincoln, 1919. New York: Houghton, Mifflin Publishing Co., 1919. NYP

DUBOIS, W.E.B. The Star of Ethiopia, (pageant), 1913.

DUDLEY, S.H., and Troy, Henry. Dr. Beans From Boston, (musical), 1911-12.

EASTON, William E. Christophe; A Tragedy in Prose of Imperial Haiti. Los Angeles: Grafton, 1911. Schom

GALE, Beresford. The Hand of Fate; or, Fifty Years After. Nashville, Tennessee: A.M.E. Sunday School Union, 1919(?). Schom

GILMORE, F. Grant. The Problem. Rochester, New York: H. Connolly, 1915. NYP

GRIMKE, Angelina. Rachel, 1916. Boston: The Cornhill Co., 1920. Schom

HANSFORD, Edwin. His Honor, the Barber, (musical), 1911.

HARPER, H.R. Tallaboo, (unprod.?), 1911.

HILL, Leubrie, and Rogers, Alex. Dark Town Follies, (musical), 1913.

HILL, J. Leubrie, and LeBaron, William. Hello Paris, (musical), 1911.
    In Best Plays of 1909-1919, Mantle, Burns. PAL

JOPLIN, Scott. Treemonisha, (opera), (unprod.), 1911.

LANDMAN, Michael. Pride of Race, 1916. In Physical Culture, Vol.
    35, (March & April, 1916). NYP

LEBARON, William, and Hill, J. Leubrie. Hello Paris, (musical), 1911.
    In Best Plays of 1909-1919, Mantle, Burns. PAL

LONGUIRE, R.B. Mammy Jinny's White Folks, (unprod.), 1915.

LYTTLETON, E. Nyanysa, (unprod.), 1911.

MIDDLETON, George. The Black Tie, (one act). In Possession and
    Other One-Act Plays, Middleton, G. New York: Henry
    Holt & Co., 1915. NYP

NELSON, Alice D. Mine Eyes Have Seen, (one act). In Crisis,
    (April, 1918).

O'NEILL, Eugene. The Moon of the Caribbees, (one act), 1918.
    London: J. Cape, 1923. NYP

O'NEILL, Eugene. Thirst, (one act), 1916. In Thirst and Other One Act
    Plays. Boston: The Gorham Press, 1914. PAL

PARENTEAU, Z. and Connolly, M. Amber Empress, (operatic comedy),
    1916. In Best Plays of 1909-19, Mantle, Burns. PAL

PENDLETON, V.H. Mammy Lucindy, Gin'l Managuh, (unprod.), 1911.

ROGERS, Alex C. Baby Blues, (musical), 1919.

ROGERS, Alex, and Hill, Leubrie. Dark Town Follies, (musical), 1913.

ROGERS, Alexander, and Creamer, Henry. The Old Man's Boy,
    (musical), 1914.

ROGERS, Alex. This and That, (musical), 1919.

ROGERS, Alex, and Creamer, Henry. The Traitor, (musical), 1912.

STEPHENS, T.W. Three Wishes. In Plays for Men. Boston: 1918.

TANNER, William H. The Birth of Freedom and the Present Age.
   Dayton, Ohio: 1919.

THOMAS, Augustus. Come Out of the Kitchen, 1916. New York:
   Samuel French, 1916. NYP

TILLMAN, Katherine David. Fifty Years of Freedom; or, From Cabin
   to Congress. Philadelphia: A.M.E. Book Concern, 1910. Schom

TORRENCE, Ridgley. Danse Calenda, 1919. In Theatre Arts Magazine,
   Vol. 3, No. 3, (July, 1919). PAL

TORRENCE, Ridgley. Granny Maumee, (one act), 1914. In Plays
   for a Negro Theatre. New York: Macmillan, 1917. Schom.

TORRENCE, Ridgley. The Rider of Dreams, (one act), 1917. In Plays
   for a Negro Theatre. New York: Macmillan, 1917. Schom

TORRENCE, Ridgley. Simon the Cyrenian, (one act), 1917. In Plays
   for a Negro Theatre. New York: Macmillan, 1917. Schom

TRAVERS Vale, The (?). Girl of the Sunny South, (unprod.), 1906.

TROY, Henry, and Dudley, S.H. Dr. Beans from Boston, (musical),
   1911-12.

1920 - 1929

ABBOTT, George, and Briders, Ann. Coquette, 1927. New York:
   Longmans, Green, 1928. NYP

ABBOTT, George, and Paramore, Edward. Ringside, 1928. In Best
   Plays of 1928-1929, Mantle, Burns. PAL

ADAMS, E.C.L. Potee's Gal. Columbia, South Carolina: State College,
   1929. Schom

ADE, George. Marse Covington, (one act). New York: Samuel French, 1923.
   NYP

ANDERSON, C. and Lessig, L. Black Diamonds, (one act). In Missionary
   Review of the World, Vol. 52, (Oct., 1929).

ANDERSON, Garland. Appearances, 1925. Manuscript, Film Reproduction 2-17. NYP

ANDERSON, Maxwell. Outside Looking In, 1925. Typescript. PAL

ATTERIDGE, Harold. Great Temptations, (musical), 1926. In Best Plays of 1925-1926, Mantle, Burns. PAL

BAILEY, L.C. Job's Kinfolks, (one act). In Carolina Folk Plays, Koch, Frederick (ed.). New York: Henry Holt, 1928. NYP

BASSHE, Emanuel Jo. Earth, 1927. New York: Macaulay Co., 1927. NYP

BARRY, Richard. Barefoot, 1925.

BATTLE, John T. and Perkman, William. The Bottom of the Cup, 1927. In Best Plays of 1926-27, Mantle, Burns. PAL

BELL, Charles. Elsie, (musical), 1923.

BELLEDNA, Alex. Pansy, (musical), 1929.

BONNER, Marita. Exit, an Illusion, (one act). In Crisis, 36:10, (Oct., 1929). NYP

BONNER, Marita. The Pot-Maker, (one act). In Opportunity, 5:2, (Feb., 1927). NYP

BONNER, Marita. The Purple Flower, (one act). In Crisis, 35:1, (Jan., 1928). NYP

BRADFORD, Perry. Messin' Around, (musical), 1929.

BRIDERS, Ann, and Abbott, George. Coquette, 1927. New York: Longmans, Green, 1928. NYP

BRUCE, Richard. Sahdji - An African Ballet, (one act), 1927. In Plays of Negro Life, Locke, Alain (ed.). New York: Harper, 1927. NYP

CAIN, James M. Hemp, (one act). In American Mercury, X, (April, 1927). NYP

CALDWELL, Ann. The Magnolia Lady, (musical), 1924. In Best Plays of 1924 - 1925, Mantle, Burns. PAL

CHAMBERLAIN, George, and Thomas, A.E. Lost, 1927. New York:
G.P. Putnam's Sons, 1926. NYP

CLARKE, Grant, and Leslie, Lew, and Turk, Roy. Dixie to Broadway,
(musical), 1924.

COHEN, Octavus R. Come Seven, 1920. New York: Longmans, Green,
and Co., 1927. NYP

COLTON, John, and Randolph, Clemence. Rain, 1922. Typescript. PAL

CONNELLY, Marc, and Kaufman, George. Beggar on Horseback, 1924.
Typescript. PAL/SF

CORT, Harry, and Rogers, Alex. Charlie, (musical), 1923.

CORT, Harry, and Stoddard, George, and Rogers, Alex. Go-Go,
(musical), 1923. In Best Plays of 1922-1923, Mantle, Burns. PAL

COTTER, Joseph. On the Fields of France, (one act). In Crisis,
20:2, (June, 1920). NYP

CRAVEN, Frank. The First Year, 1921. New York: Samuel French,
1921. NYP

CREAMER, Henry, and Duncan, William. Three Showers, (musical), 1920.
In Best Plays of 1919-1920, Mantle, Burns. PAL

CULBERTSON, Ernest. Goat Alley, 1921. Cincinnati: Stewart Kidd,
1922. NYP

CUNEY-HARE, Maud. Antar of Araby, (one act), 1929. In Plays
and Pageants from the Life of the Negro, Richardson, W. (ed.).
Washington, D.C.: Associated Publishers, 1930. NYP

CUSHING, Catherine. Topsy and Eva, (musical), 1924.

DAVENPORT, Butler. Justice, 1920.

DAVIS, Owen. Easy Come, Easy Go, 1925. New York: Samuel French,
1926. NYP

DAZEY, Frank, and Tully, Jim. Black Boy, 1926. In Best Plays of
1926-27, Mantle, Burns. PAL

DE LEON, Walter, and Dunn, Edward D. Under the Bamboo Tree,
(musical), 1921. Typescript. PAL

DE REATH, Irene Byrd. The Yellow Tree, 1921.

DIXON, Rev. Thomas. A Man of the People. New York: D. Appleton and
Co., 1920. NYP

DONNELLY, Dorothy. My Maryland, (musical), 1927.

DORTCH, Helen. Companion-Mate Maggie, 1929. In Carolina Folk
Comedies, Koch, Frederick, (ed.). New York: Samuel French,
1931. PAL

DOWLING, Eddie, and Hanley, James. Honeymoon Lane, (musical),
1926. In Best Plays of 1926-1927, Mantle, Burns. PAL

DOWNING, Henry F. The Racial Tangle, 1920.

DUFF, Donald, and Manley, Dorothy, and Spence, Doralyne. The
Stigma, 1927.

DUNCAN, Thelma. The Death Dance, (one act), 1923. In Plays
of Negro Life, Locke, Alain (ed.). New York: Harper, 1927.
NYP

DUNCAN, William C. and Wells, John. Great Day, (musical),
1929. In Best Plays of 1929-1930, Mantle, Burns. PAL

DUNCAN, William, and Creamer, Henry. Three Showers, (musical),
1920. In Best Plays of 1919-1920, Mantle, Burns. PAL

DUNN, Edward, and de Leon, Walter. Under the Bamboo Tree,
(musical), 1921. Typescript. PAL

EDMONDS, Randolph. Christmas Gift, (one act), (unprod.), 1923.

EDMONDS, Randolph. Denmark Vesey, (one act), (unprod.), 1929.

EDMONDS, Randolph. Doom, (one act), (unprod.), 1924.

EDMONDS, Randolph. The Highwayman, (one act), 1925.

EDMONDS, Randolph. Illicit Love, (unprod.), 1927.

EDMONDS, Randolph. Job Hunting, (one act), 1922.

EDMONDS, Randolph. A Merchant in Dixie, (one act), (unprod.), 1923.

EDMONDS, Randolph. One Side of Harlem, (unprod.), 1928.

EDMONDS, Randolph. Rocky Roads, 1926.

EDMONDS, Randolph. Silas Brown, (one act), 1927. In The Land of Cotton
and Other Plays, Edmonds, R. Washington, D.C.: Associated
Publishers, Inc., 1943. NYP

EDMONDS, Randolph. Sirlock Bones, (one act), 1928.

EDMONDS, Randolph. Stock Exchange, (musical), (unprod.), 1927.

EDMONDS, Randolph. Takazee - A Pageant of Ethiopia, 1928.

EDMONDS, Randolph. The Virginia Politician, (unprod.), (one act),
1927.

EVANS, Margaret. Faith, (one act). In Poet Lore, Vol. 33,
(Spring, 1922).

FERBER, Edna and Kaufman, George. Minick, 1924. Garden City,
New York: Doubleday Page & Co., 1924. NYP

FERBER, Edna, and Kaufman, George S. The Royal Family, 1927.
Garden City, N.Y.: Doubleday, Doran, & Co., 1928. NYP

FIELDS, Dorothy, and Leslie, Lew. Blackbirds of 1928, (musical),
1928.

FLAVIN, Martin. The Criminal Code, 1929. New York: H.
Liveright, 1930. NYP

FLAVIN, Martin. Cross Roads, 1929. New York: Samuel French,
1930. NYP

FLINT, Eva Kay, and Madison, Martha. Subway Express, 1929.
Typescript. PAL

FROST, Walter A. Cape Smoke, 1925. In Best Plays of 1924-1925,
Mantle, Burns. PAL

GAINES-SHELTCN, Ruth. The Church Fight, (one act). In
Crisis, 32:1, (May, 1926). NYP

GARDINER, Becky, and Veiller, Bayard. Damn Your Honor, 1929. In
Best Plays of 1929-1930, Mantle, Burns. PAL

GILES, William, and Giles, Josephine. Gabe's Home Run, (one act).
In Plays, Rein, A.E. (ed.). Milwaukee, Wis.: A.E. Rein, n.d.

GOLD, Michael. Hoboken Blues (subtitled The Black Rip Van Winkle), 1926. In The American Caravan, Van Wyck, Brooks (ed.). New York: Macaulay, 1927. Schom

GORDON, Leon. White Cargo, 1923. Boston: The Four Seas Co., 1925. NYP

GRAHAM, Ottie. Holiday, (one act). In Crisis, 26:1, (May, 1923). NYP

GRAINGER, Porter, & Whipper, Leigh. De Board Meetin', (one act), 1925. Typescript. Schom

GRAINGER, Porter, and Johnson, Freddie. Lucky Sambo, (musical), 1925. In Best Plays of 1925-26, Mantle, Burns. PAL

GRAINGER, Porter, and Whipper, Leigh. We's Risin', (musical), 1927. Typescript. Schom

GREEN, Paul. In Abraham's Bosom, (one act), 1924. New York: Harper & Bros., 1927.

GREEN, Paul. In Abraham's Bosom (in seven scenes), 1926. Typescript. PAL

GREEN, Paul. Blackbeard, (one act), 1921. In The Lord's Will and Other Carolina Plays. New York: Henry Holt & Co., 1925. NYP

GREEN, Paul. Blue Thunder, (one act). In One Act Plays for Stage and Study, third series. New York: Samuel French, 1928. PAL

GREEN, Paul. The End of the Row, (one act), 1923. In Lonesome Road, Clark, B., (ed.). New York: B.M. McBride & Co., 1926. NYP

GREEN, Paul. The Goodbye, (one act). In In The Valley and Other Carolina Plays. New York: Samuel French, 1928. NYP

GREEN, Paul. The Hot Iron, (one act), 1923. In Out of the South. New York: Harper & Bros., 1939. NYP

GREEN, Paul. In Aunt Mahaly's Cabin, (one act), 1924. New York: Samuel French, 1925. NYP

GREEN, Paul. In the Valley, (one act), 1927. In In the Valley and Other Carolina Plays. New York: Samuel French, 1928. NYP

GREEN, Paul. Last of the Lowries, (one act), 1920. New York: Samuel French, 1922. NYP

GREEN, Paul. The Man on the House, (one act), 1926. In In the Valley and Other Carolina Plays. New York: Samuel French, 1928. NYP

GREEN, Paul. The Man Who Died at Twelve O'Clock, (one act), 1923. In In The Valley and Other Carolina Plays. New York: Samuel French, 1928. NYP

GREEN, Paul. No 'Count Boy, (one act), 1923. In In the Valley and Other Carolina Plays. New York: Samuel French, 1928. NYP

GREEN, Paul. The Old Man of Edenton, (one act), 1920. In The Lord's Will and Other Carolina Plays. New York: Henry Holt & Co., 1925. NYP

GREEN, Paul. Old Wash Lucas. New York: Henry Holt, 1924.

GREEN, Paul. The Prayer Meeting (Granny Boling, 1921 - revised), (one act), 1923. In Lonesome Road, Clark, B., (ed.). New York: R.M. McBride & Co., 1926. NYP

GREEN, Paul. Son-Boy, (one act). In Saturday Evening Quill, Boston, (June, 1928).

GREEN, Paul. Supper for the Dead, (one act), 1926. In In the Valley and Other Carolina Plays. New York: Samuel French, 1928. NYP

GREEN, Paul. White Dresses, (one act), 1920. In Lonesome Road, Clark, B., (ed.). New York: R.M. McBride & Co., 1926. NYP

GREEN, Paul. Your Fiery Furnace, (Sam Tucker - revised), (one act), 1921. In Lonesome Road, Clark, B., (ed.). New York: R.M. McBride & Co., 1926. NYP

GREENE, H.C. Just a Minute, (musical), 1928. In Best Plays of 1928-1929, Mantle, Burns. PAL

GUINN, Dorothy C. Out of the Dark, (pageant), 1924. In Plays
and Pageants from the Life of the Negro, Richardson, W. (ed.).
Washington, D.C.: Associated Publishers, 1930. NYP

GYNT, Kaj, and Trent, Jo. Rang Tang, (musical), 1927.

HAMMERSTEIN, Oscar II, and Harbach, Otto. Golden Dawn,
(musical), 1927. In Best Plays of 1927-1928, Mantle, Burns.
PAL

HAMMERSTEIN, Oscar. Showboat, (musical), 1927. London:
Chappell & Co., 1934.

HANLEY, James, and Dowling, Eddie. Honeymoon Lane, (musical),
1926. In Best Plays of 1926-1927, Mantle, Burns. PAL

HARBACH, Otto, and Hammerstein, Oscar II. Golden Dawn,
(musical), 1927. In Best Plays of 1927-1928, Mantle, Burns.
PAL

HARTLEY, Roland E. and Power, Caroline. Madame Delphine,
(one act). In Short Plays from Great Stories, Hartley and
Power. New York: Macmillan Co., 1928.

HECHT, Ben, & MacArthur, Charles. The Front Page, 1928.
New York: Covici-Friede, 1933. NYP/SF

HEYWOOD, DuBose and Dorothy. Porgy, 1927. New York:
Doubleday Page & Co., 1927.

HILL, Leslie P. Toussaint L'Ouverture. Boston: Christopher Publishing
Co., 1928. NYP

HORAN, Charles. The Devil Within, 1925. In Best Plays of 1924-1925,
Mantle, Burns. PAL

HUGHES, Langston. The Gold Piece, (unprod.), 1921.

HUNTER, Eddie. How Come?, 1923. In Best Plays of 1922-1923,
Mantle, Burns. PAL

HUNTER, Eddie, and Rogers, Alex. My Magnolia, (musical), 1926.

HURSTON, Zora N. Great Day, 1927.

HUTTY, Leigh. House of Shadows, 1927. In Best Plays of 1926-1927,
Mantle, Burns. PAL

HYMER, John, and Shipman, Samuel. Fast Life, 1928. In Best
Plays of 1928-1929, Mantle, Burns. PAL

JEFFERSON, W.J. Mandy, (one act), 1926.

JOHNSON, Fenton. The Cabaret Girl, 1925.

JOHNSON, Freddie, and Grainger, Porter. Lucky Sambo, (musical),
1925. In Best Plays of 1925-26, Mantle, Burns. PAL

JOHNSON, Georgia D. Blue Blood, (one act). In Fifty More
Contemporary One Act Plays, Shay, Frank (ed.). New York:
Appleton, 1928. NYP

JOHNSON, Georgia D. Plumes, (one act). In Plays of
Negro Life, Locke, Alain (ed.). New York:
Harper, 1927. NYP

KAUFMAN, George and Connelly, Marc. Beggar on Horseback,
1924. Typescript. PAL/SF

KAUFMAN, George and Ferber, Edna. Minick, 1924. Garden
City, New York: Doubleday Page & Co., 1924. NYP

KAUFMAN, George S., and Ferber, Edna. The Royal Family,
1927. Garden City, N.Y.: Doubleday, Doran, & Co.,
1928. NYP/SF

KAVANAUGH, Katharine. The Ghost Parade, 1929. Chicago:
The Dramatic Publishing Co., 1929. NYP

KENNEDY, Harriet. The Lion's Mouth. New York: D. Appleton
and Co., 1924. NYP

KRENEK, Ernst. Jonny Spielt Auf, (jazz opera), 1929.

LAWSON, John Howard. Processional, 1925. New York:
T. Seltzer, 1925. NYP (Revised FTP-1937-PAL)

LAYTON, J. and Creamer, Henry. Strut Miss Lizzie, (musical),
1922.

LESLIE, Lew, and Fields, Dorothy. Blackbirds of 1928, (musical),
1928.

LESLIE, Lew, and Turk, Roy, and Clarke, Grant. Dixie to Broadway,
(musical), 1924.

LESLIE, Lew, and Turk, Roy. The Plantation Revue, (musical), 1922. In Best Plays of 1922-1923, Mantle, Burns. PAL

LESSIG, L. and Anderson, C. Black Diamonds, (one act). In Missionary Review of the World, Vol. 52, (Oct., 1929).

LIPSCOMB, C.D. Frances, (one act). In Opportunity, 3:29, (May, 1925). NYP

LIVINGSTON, Myrtle A. For Unborn Children, (one act). In Crisis, 32:3, (July, 1926). NYP

LYLES, Aubrey and Miller, Flournoy. Keep Shufflin', (musical), 1928.

LYLES, Aubrey and Miller, Flournoy. Runnin' Wild, (musical), 1923.

LYLES, Aubrey, and Miller, Flournoy. Shuffle Along, (musical), 1921.

MACARTHUR, Charles, and Hecht, Ben. The Front Page, 1928. New York: Covici-Friede, 1933. NYP/SF

MACARTHUR, Charles and Sheldon, Edward. Lula Belle, 1926. In Best Plays of 1925-26, Mantle, Burns. PAL

MCCOO, Edward. Ethiopia at the Bar of Justice, (one act), 1924. In Plays and Pageants from the Life of the Negro, Richardson, W. (ed.). Washington, D.C.: Associated Publishers, 1930. NYP

MCENVOY, J.P. God Loves Us, 1926. Typescript. PAL

MACK, Willard. Weather Clear - Track Fast, 1927. Typescript. PAL

MADISON, Martha, and Flint, Eva Kay. Subway Express, 1929. Typescript. PAL

MANLEY, Dorothy, and Spence, Doralyne, and Duff, Donald. Stigma, 1927.

MARCUS, Frank. Bamboola, (musical), 1929.

MARCUS, Frank. Make Me Know It, 1929. In Best Plays of 1929-30, Mantle, Burns. PAL

MATHEUS, John. Black Damp, (one act). In Caroline Magazine, 49, (April, 1929).

MATHEUS, John. 'Cruiter, (one act), 1926. In Plays of Negro Life, Locke, Alain (ed.). New York: Harper, 1927. NYP

MATHEUS, John. Ti Yette, (one act), 1929. In Plays and Pageants from the Life of the Negro, Richardson, W. (ed.). Washington, D.C.: Associated Publishers, 1930. NYP

MILLER, Allen C. The Opener of Doors. In Negro One Act Plays, Vol. 40, 1923. Partial publication of longer play.

MILLER, Flournoy, et.al. Brownskin Models, (musical), 1927.

MILLER, Flournoy, and Lyles, Aubrey. Keep Shufflin', (musical), 1928.

MILLER, Flournoy, and Lyles, Aubrey. Runnin' Wild, (musical), 1923.

MILLER, Flournoy, and Lyles, Aubrey. Shuffle Along, (musical), 1921.

MILLER, Irvin, and Pinkard, Maceo. Liza, (musical), 1922. In Best Plays of 1922-1923, Mantle, Burns. PAL

MILLER, Irvin C. Put and Take, (musical), 1921.

MILLER, J.C. Dinah, 1924.

MILLER, May. Scratches, (one act). In Carolina Magazine, 49, (April, 1929).

MORGAN, Edwin J. The Return, 1920.

MORTIMER, Lillian. Mammy's Lil' Wild Rose. Chicago: T.S. Demson & Co., 1924. NYP

MULLALLY, Don. Wanted, 1928. In Best Plays of 1928-1929, Mantle, Burns. PAL

MYGATT, Tracy. The Noose, (one act). In Drama, XX (Nov., 1929).

NUGENT, John C., and Nugent, Elliott. By Request, 1928.

O'NEILL, Eugene. All God's Chillun Got Wings, 1924. New York: Boni & Liveright, 1924. NYP/DPS

O'NEILL, Eugene. The Dreamy Kid, (one act), 1919. In Plays of Negro Life, Locke, Alain (ed.). New York: Harper, 1927. NYP

O'NEILL, Eugene. The Emperor Jones, (one act), 1920. New York: Boni & Liveright, 1921. NYP/DPS

OVINGTON, Mary White. The Awakening. New York: NAACP, 1923. Schom

PARAMORE, Edward, and Abbott, George. Ringside, 1928. In Best Plays of 1928-1929, Mantle, Burns. PAL

PAYTON, Lew, and Sissle, Noble. Chocolate Dandies, (musical), 1924.

PERKMAN, William, and Battle, John T. The Bottom of the Cup, 1927. In Best Plays of 1926-27. Mantle, Burns. PAL

PINKARD, Maceo, and Miller, Irvin. Liza, (musical), 1922. In Best Plays of 1922-1923, Mantle, Burns. PAL

POWER, Caroline, and Hartley, Roland E. Madame Delphine, (one act). In Short Plays from Great Stories, Hartley and Power. New York: MacMillan Co., 1928.

RANDOLPH, Clemence, and Colton, John. Rain, 1922. Typescript. PAL

RAPP, W.S., and Thurman, Wallace. Harlem, 1929. Typescript. YL

RAZAF, Andy. Hot Chocolates, (musical), 1929.

RICHARDSON, Willis. The Black Horseman, (one act), 1929. In Plays and Pageants from the Life of the Negro, Richardson, Willis (ed.). Washington, D.C.: Associated Publishers, 1930. Schom

RICHARDSON, Willis. The Bootblack Lover, (unprod.), 1926.

RICHARDSON, Willis. The Broken Banjo, (one act), 1925. In Plays of Negro Life, Locke, Alain (ed.). New York: Harper, 1927. Schom

RICHARDSON, Willis. The Chip Woman's Fortune, (one act), 1923. In Anthology of the American Negro in the Theatre, Patterson, Lindsay (ed.). New York: The Publishers Co., 1967. PAL

RICHARDSON, Willis. Compromise, (one act), 1926. In The New Negro, Locke, Alain (ed.). New York: Albert and Charles Boni, 1925. Schom

RICHARDSON, Willis. The Deacon's Awakening, (one act), 1921. In Crisis, Nov. 1920. NYP

RICHARDSON, Willis. The Flight of the Natives, (one act), 1927. In
Plays of Negro Life, Locke, Alain (ed.). New York: Harper, 1927.

RICHARDSON, Willis. The House of Sham, (one act), 1928. In Plays
and Pageants from the Life of the Negro, Richardson, Willis (ed.).
Washington, D.C.: Associated Publishers, 1930. Schom

RICHARDSON, Willis. The Idle Head, (one act). In Carolina
Magazine, (April, 1929).

RICHARDSON, Willis. The King's Dilemma, (one act), 1929. In
The King's Dilemma and Other Plays for Children. New York:
Exposition Press, 1956. Schom

RICHARDSON, Willis. Mortgaged, (one act), 1924. In Readings from
Negro Authors, Cromwell & Dykes & Fuller (eds.). New York:
Harcourt, 1931.

RICHARDSON, Willis. The Peacock's Feathers, (one act), 1928.
Typescript. Schom

RIDEOUT, Ransom. Goin' Home, 1928. New York: Longmans, Green
& Co., 1928. NYP

ROBERTSON, Willard. Black Velvet, 1927. In Best Plays of 1927-28,
Mantle, Burns. PAL

ROGERS, Alex, and Cort, Harry. Charlie, (musical), 1923.

ROGERS, Alex, and Cort, Harry, and Stoddard, George. Go-Go,
(musical), 1923. In Best Plays of 1922-1923, Mantle, Burns. PAL

ROGERS, Alex, and Hunter, Eddie. My Magnolia, (musical), 1926.

ROGERS, J.W. Judge Lynch, (one act), 1924. In Plays of Negro Life,
Locke, Alain (ed.). New York: Harper, 1927. NYP

SABATINI, Rafael, and Terry, Harold. The Carolinian, 1925. In Best
Plays of 1925-1926, Mantle, Burns. PAL

ST. CLAIR, Stewart. Lace Petticoat, (musical), 1927. In Best Plays of
1926-1927, Mantle, Burns. PAL

SCOTT, Natalie V. Zombi. In Plays of American Life and Fantasy,
Isaacs, E. (ed.). New York: Coward-McCann, 1929. NYP

39

SHELDON, Edward, and MacArthur, Charles. Lula Belle, 1926. In Best Plays of 1925-26, Mantle, Burns. PAL

SHERMAN, Robert J. Spooks, 1925. Typescript. PAL

SHIPMAN, Samuel, and Hymer, John. Fast Life, 1928. In Best Plays of 1928-1929, Mantle, Burns. PAL

SHORT, Marion. Rose of the Southland. New York: Samuel French, 1924. NYP

SISSLE, Noble, and Payton, Lew. Chocolate Dandies, (musical), 1924.

SMITH, Edgar, and Young, Emily. Red Pepper, (musical), 1922.

SPENCE, Doralyne, and Manley, Dorothy, and Buff, Donald. Stigma, 1927.

SPENCE, Eulalie. Foreign Mail, (one act), 1927. New York: Samuel French, 1927.

SPENCE, Eulalie. Fool's Errand, (one act). New York: Samuel French, 1927. FTP

SPENCE, Eulalie. Help Wanted. In Saturday Evening Quill, Boston, (April, 1929.) NYP

SPENCE, Eulalie. Her, (one act), 1927.

SPENCE, Eulalie. The Hunch, (one act), (unprod.), 1927.

SPENCE, Eulalie. The Starter, (one act). In Plays of Negro Life, Locke, Alain (ed.). New York: Harper, 1927. NYP

SPENCE, Eulalie. Undertow, (one act). In Caroline Magazine, 49, (April, 1929).

STALLINGS, Lawrence. Deep River, (opera), 1926. In Best Plays of 1926-27, Mantle, Burns. PAL

STEPHENS, Nan Bagby. Charivari, (one act), 1928. In Plays of American Life and Fantasy, Isaacs, E. (ed.). New York: Coward-McCann, Inc., 1929. NYP

STEPHENS, Nan Bagby. Roseanne, 1923. In Best Plays of 1923-24, Mantle, Burns. PAL

STODDARD, George, Crot, Harry, and Rogers, Alex. Go-Go, (musical), 1923. In Best Plays of 1922-1923, Mantle, Burns. PAL

SUTHERLAND, Evelyn G. In Aunt Chloe's Cabin. Boston: W.H. Baker and Co., 1925. NYP

TARKINGTON, Booth. Magnolia, 1923. In Best Plays of 1923-1924, Mantle, Burns. PAL

TERRY, Harold, and Sabatini, Rafael. The Carolinian, 1925. In Best Plays of 1925-1926, Mantle, Burns. PAL

THOMAS, A.E. and Chamberlain, George. Lost, 1927. New York: G.P. Putnam's Sons, 1926. NYP

THOMPSON, Eloise Bibb. Caught, 1925. In Best Plays of 1925-1926, Mantle, Burns. PAL

THOMPSON, Eloise Bibb. Cooped Up, 1924.

THORNE, David. Beyond Evil, 1926. In Best Plays of 1925-1926, Mantle, Burns. PAL

THURMAN, Wallace, and Rapp, W.J. Harlem, 1929. Typescript. YL

TOOMER, Jean. Balo, (one act), 1927. In Plays of Negro Life, Locke, Alain (ed.). New York: Harper, 1927. NYP

TOOMER, Jean. Kabnis. In Cane, Toomer, J. New York: Boni and Liveright, 1923. Schom

TUCKER, Clyde. Matrimony Up-To-Date, (one act). In Banner Anthology of One-Act Plays by American Authors, Carter, L.H. (ed.). San Francisco: 1929.

TULLY, Jim and Dazey, Frank. Black Boy, 1926. In Best Plays of 1926-27, Mantle, Burns. PAL

TURK, Roy, and Clarke, Grant, and Leslie, Lew. Dixie to Broadway, (musical), 1924.

TURK, Roy, and Leslie, Lew. The Plantation Revue, (musical), 1922. In Best Plays of 1922-1923, Mantle, Burns. PAL

TUTT, Homer, and Whitney, Salem. Deep Harlem, (musical), 1929.

VEILLER, Bayard. The Trial of Mary Dugan, 1927. New York:
Samuel French, 1928. NYP

VEILLER, Bayard, and Gardiner, Becky. Damn Your Honor, 1929.
In Best Plays of 1929-1930, Mantle, Burns. PAL

VODERY, William. Blue Monday, (opera ala Afro-American), 1922.

WARE, Alice. The Open Door, (pageant), 1923.

WELLS, John, and Duncan, William. Great Day, (musical), 1929.
In Best Plays of 1929-1930, Mantle, Burns. PAL

WEST, Mae. Pleasure Man, 1928. In Best Plays of 1928-1929,
Mantle, Burns. PAL

WHIPPER, Leigh, and Grainger, Porter. De Board Meetin', (one act),
1925. Typescript. Schom

WHIPPER, Leigh, and Grainger, Porter. We's Risin', (musical), 1927.
Typescript. Schom

WHITE, Lucy. The Bird Child, (one act), 1922. In Plays of Negro Life,
Locke, Alain (ed.). New York: Harper, 1927. NYP

WHITNEY, Salem, and Tutt, Homer. Deep Harlem, (musical), 1929.

WIBORG, May Hoyt. Taboo, 1922. In Best Plays of 1921-22, Mantle,
Burns. PAL

WILLARD, John. The Cat and the Canary, 1922. In Best Plays of
1921-1922, Mantle, Burns. PAL

WILLIAMS, Clarence. Bottomland, (musical), 1927. In Best Plays
of 1927-1928, Mantle, Burns. PAL

WILSON, Frank H. Confidence, (one act), 1922.

WILSON, Frank. Meek Mose, 1928. In Best Plays of 1927-28,
Mantle, Burns. PAL

WILSON, Frank. Sugar Cane, (one act). In Opportunity 4:6,
(June, 1926). NYP

YATES, Elizabeth H. The Slave, (one act). In Small Plays for Small
Casts. Philadelphia: Penn Publishing Co., 1926. NYP

YOUNG, Emily, and Smith, Edgar. Red Pepper, (musical), 1922.

1930 - 1939

ABBOTT, George. Sweet River, (musical), 1936. Prompt book. PAL

ABBOTT, George, and Holm, John. Three Men on a Horse, 1935.
    New York: Dramatists Play Service, 1937. NYP

ALBRIGHT, Hardie. All the Living, 1938. Typescript. PAL

ALEXANDER, Leon, and Hayes, Alfred. Journeyman, 1938.
    Typescript. PAL

ALLEN, James. The Wind Blows, (one act). In One Act Play
    Magazine, (March, 1939). PAL

ALLISON, Hughes. The Trial of Dr. Beck, 1937. In Best Plays of
    1937-38, Mantle, Burns. PAL

AMES, Christine, and Clarke, Painter. Black Empire, 1936. FTP

ANDERSON, Maxwell. Both Your Houses, 1933. New York:
    Samuel French, 1933. NYP

ANDERSON, Maxwell. The Wingless Victory, 1936. Washington, D.C.:
    Anderson House, 1936. NYP

ANDREWS, Regina. Underground, (one act), 1933(?).

ANGUS, Bernie. Brown Sugar (Home Sweet Harlem), 1937.
    Typescript. PAL

ANONYMOUS. Mojo, 193? Typescript. PAL

ARENT, Arthur. Ethiopia, (unprod.), 1936.

ARENT, Arthur. 1935 (Living Newspaper). Typescript. FTP. PAL

ARENT, Arthur. One-Third of a Nation. New York: Random House,
    1938. FTP. NYP

ASHLEY, William. Booker T. Washington, 1939.

ATLAS, Leopold. But For the Grace of God, 1937. New York:
    Samuel French, 1937. NYP

43

BAILEY, Rietta. Mourners to Glory, (one act). In American Folk
    Plays, Koch, Frederick (ed.). New York: D. Appleton-Century Co.,
    1939. NYP

BAILEY, Rietta. Washed in de Blood, (one act), 1937. In International
    Folk Plays, Selden, Samuel (ed.). Chapel Hill: University
    Press, 1949. NYP

BARKER, Eulalie. Ambiguity, (one act), 1931(?)

BARTON, Arthur, and Chodorov, Edward. Wonder Boy, 1931. In
    Best Plays of 1931-1932, Mantle, Burns. PAL

BECKWITH, Russell, and Courtney, Ward. Mango, 1937. FTP

BEHRMAN, S.N. No Time for Comedy, 1939. New York: Random House,
    1939. NYP

BENNETT, Dorothy, and Hannah, Link. Woman's A Fool to be Clever,
    1938. New York: Samuel French, 1939. NYP

BENNETT, Isadora. The Soon Bright Day, 193? Typescript. Schom

BERLIN, Irving, and Hart, Moss. Face the Music, 1932. In Best
    Plays of 1931-1932, Mantle, Burns. PAL

BLANKFORT, Michael and Gold, Michael. Battle Hymn, 1936. New
    York: Samuel French, 1936. FTP

BOND, Frederick W. Family Affair. In Institute, West Virginia:
    West Virginia State College, 1939.

BONTEMPS, Arna, and Hughes, Langston. When the Jack Hollars.
    Microfilm, 1936. Schom

BOOTHE, Clare. Kiss the Boys Goodbye, 1938. New York: Random
    House, 1939. NYP

BRADFORD, Roark and Connelly, Marc. Green Pastures, 1930. New
    York: Farrar, 1957. DPS NYP

BRADFORD, Roark, and Connelly, Marc. Little David, (one act).
    New York: Dramatists Play Service, 1937. NYP

BRADFORD, Roark. How Come Christmas, (one act). New York:
    Harper & Bros., 1930. NYP

BRENNAN, Frederick H. Stick-In-The-Mud, 1935. Typescript. PAL

BROWN, Beth, and Shipman, Samuel. Behind Red Lights, 1937.
Typescript. PAL

BROWN, Chamberlain. Chamberlain Brown's Scrap Book, 1932. In
Best Plays of 1932-1933, Mantle, Burns. PAL

BROWN, Lew, and Henderson, Ray. Strike Me Pink, 1933. In
Best Plays of 1932-1933, Mantle, Burns. PAL

BROWNE, Theodore. The Natural Man, 1936. Promptbook, 1937.
FTP. PAL

BROWNELL, John C. Mississippi Rainbow (Brainsweat), 1934. New York:
Samuel French, 1935. NYP

BRUCE, Richard, and McClendon, Rose. Taxi Fare, (one act), 1931.

BRYANT, George. Second Comin', 1931. In Best Plays of 1931-32,
Mantle, Burns. PAL

BULLOCH, Turner. Lady of Letters, 1935. New York: Samuel
French, 1935. NYP

BURKE, Inez. Two Races, (pageant), 1930. In Plays and Pageants from
the Life of the Negro, Richardson, W. (ed.). Washington, D.C.:
Associated Publishers, 1930. NYP

BUTLER, Frank, and Raine, Norman. Hangman's Whip, 1933. In Best
Plays of 1932-1933, Mantle, Burns. PAL

BUTTITTA, Anthony. Singing Piedmont, (one act). In One Act Play
Magazine Annual Anthology, 1937-1938. New York: Contemporary
Play Publishers, 1938. PAL

CAMPBELL, Lawson. Solid South, 1930. New York: Samuel French,
1931. NYP

CHARELL, Eric, and Selders, Gilbert. Swingin' The Dream, (musical),
1939. FTP

CHODOROV, Edward, and Barton, Arthur. Wonder Boy, 1931. In Best
Plays of 1931-1932, Mantle, Burns. PAL

CHORPENNING, Charolette. Little Black Sambo and the Tigers, 1939(?)
New York: Dramatists Play Service, 1938. PAL

CLARKE, Harry. A Little Racketeer, (musical), 1932. In Best Plays of 1931-1932, Mantle, Burns. PAL

CLARKE, Painter and Ames, Christine. Black Empire, 1936. FTP

CONNELLY, Marc and Bradford, Roark. Green Pastures, 1930. New York: Farrar, 1957. DPS NYP

CONNELLY, Marc and Bradford, Roark. Little David, (one act). New York: Dramatists Play Service, 1937. NYP

COOK, Alice Carter. Komateekay, (one act). Boston: Bruce Humphries, Inc., 1936. NYP

COURLANDER, Harold. Home to Langford County, (one act). Troy, Michigan: The Blue Ox Press, 1938. NYP

COURLANDER, Harold. Swamp Mud, 1931. Detroit: M.S. Kaplan, 1936. NYP

COURTNEY, Ward, and Beckwith, Russell. Mango, 1937. FTP

COWARD, Noel. Set to Music, 1936. In Best Plays of 1938-1939, Mantle, Burns. PAL

CRITHERSPOON, Kathleen. Jute, 1937.

CULBERTSON, Ernest H. Color In Court, (one act). New York: Samuel French, 1933. NYP

CULLEN, Countee. Medea. New York: Harper & Bros., 1935. NYP

CULLEN, Countee. One Way to Heaven. Manuscript, 1936? YL

DAFORA, Asadata. Kykunkor, (dance opera), 1934. In Best Plays of 1933-1934, Mantle, Burns. PAL

DATALLER, Roger and Eaglestone, Archibald. Prince of Obolo, (one act), 1934. London: J.M. Dent and Co., 1934. NYP

DAVIS, Bernard. Dark Corner, 1938(?) FTP

DAVIS, Nellie L. Heaven Bound, 1932.

DAVIS, Owen. Jezebel, 1933. In Best Plays of 1933-1934, Mantle, Burns. PAL

DAVIS, Owen. Too Many Boats, 1934. In Best Plays of 1934-1935, Mantle, Burns. PAL

DAVIS, Owen, and Stallings, Laurence. Virginia, (musical), 1937. In Best Plays of 1937-1938, Mantle, Burns. PAL

DIETZ, Howard, and Schwartz, Arthur. At Home Abroad, (musical), 1935. In Best Plays of 1934-1935, Mantle, Burns. PAL

DODSON, Owen. Amistad, 1939. Manuscript. YL

DODSON, Owen. Divine Comedy, 1938. Manuscript. YL

DODSON, Owen. The Garden of Time (Athens, Georgia), 1939. Manuscript, YL

DODSON, Owen. Gargoyles in Florida, (one act), (unprod.), 1936.

DODSON, Owen. Including Laughter, 1936. Manuscript. YL

DONOGHUE, Dennis and Dumore, James. The Black Messiah, 1939. In Best Plays of 1938-39, Mantle, Burns. PAL

DONOGHUE, Dennis. Legal Murder, 1934. In Best Plays of 1933-34, Mantle, Burns. PAL

DORFMAN, Nat, and Leslie, Lew, and Holiner, Mann. Blackbirds of 1933, (musical), 1933.

DORSEY, Robert. Get Thee Behind Me, Satan, (one act), 1931.

DORSEY, Robert. Waxen Lily, (one act), 1933?

DOWDY, Jameson B. Light and Shadow, (one act). Chicago: T.S. Dennison & Co., 1939.

DRANSFIELD, Jane. Blood of Kings, (one act). In The American Scene, Clark & Nicholson (eds.). New York: D. Appleton & Co., 1930. NYP

DUBOIS, William. Haiti, 1938. New York: Random House, 1938. PAL

DUBOIS, William and Ricardel, Molly. I Love You Wednesday, 1932. Typescript. PAL

DUBOIS, William. Michael Drops In, 1938. In Best Plays of 1938-1939, Mantle, Burns. PAL

DUMORE, James, and Donoghue, Dennis. The Black Messiah, 1939. In Best Plays of 1938-39, Mantle, Burns. PAL

DUNCAN, Thelma. Black Magic, (one act). In The Yearbook of Short Plays, First Series. Wise and Snook (eds.). Evanston, Ill.: Rowe Peterson, 1931. NYP

DUNCAN, Thelma. Sacrifice, (one act). Plays and Pageants from the Life of the Negro, Richardson, Willis (ed.). Washington, D.C.: Associated Publishers, 1930. Schom

EAGLESTONE, Archibald and Dataller, Roger. Prince of Obolo, (one act), 1934. London: J.M. Dent and Co., 1934. NYP

EDMONDS, Randolph. Bad Man, (one act). In Six Plays for a Negro Theatre, Edmonds, R. Boston: Walter Baker, 1934. NYP

EDMONDS, Randolph. Bleeding Hearts, (one act). In Six Plays for a Negro Theatre, Edmonds, R. Boston: Walter Baker, 1934. NYP

EDMONDS, Randolph. The Breeders, (one act). In Six Plays for a Negro Theatre, Edmonds, R. Boston: Walter Baker, 1934. NYP

EDMONDS, Randolph. The Call of Jubah, (one act), (unprod.), 1935.

EDMONDS, Randolph. The Devil's Price, (one act). In Shades and Shadows, Edmonds, R. Boston: Meador Publishing Co., 1930. NYP

EDMONDS, Randolph. Drama Enters the Curriculum (A Purpose Play), (one act), 1930.

EDMONDS, Randolph. Everyman's Land, (one act). In Shades and Shadows, Edmonds, R. Boston: Meador Publishing Co., 1930. NYP

EDMONDS, Randolph. For Fatherland, (one act), 1934.

EDMONDS, Randolph. Gangsters Over Harlem, (one act), 1939. In The Land of Cotton and Other Plays, Edmonds, R. Washington, D.C.: Associated Publishers, Inc., 1943. NYP

EDMONDS, Randolph. Hewers of Wood, (one act). In Shades and Shadows, Edmonds, R. Boston: Meador Publishing Co., 1930. NYP

EDMONDS, Randolph. The High Court of Historia, (one act), 1939. In The Land of Cotton and Other Plays, Edmonds, R. Washington, D.C.: Associated Publishers, Inc., 1943. NYP

EDMONDS, Randolph. The Man of God, (unprod.), 1931.

EDMONDS, Randolph. Nat Turner, (one act). In Six Plays for
a Negro Theatre, Edmonds, R. Boston: Walter Baker, 1934. NYP

EDMONDS, Randolph. The New Window, (one act). In Six Plays
for a Negro Theatre, Edmonds, R. Boston: Walter Baker, 1934.
NYP

EDMONDS, Randolph. Old Man Pete, (one act). In Six
Plays for a Negro Theatre, Edmonds, R. Boston: Walter
Baker, 1934. NYP

EDMONDS, Randolph. The Outer Room, (one act), (unprod.), 1935.

EDMONDS, Randolph. Peter Stith, (one act), 1933.

EDMONDS, Randolph. The Phantom Treasure. In Shades and
Shadows, Edmonds, R. Boston: Meador Publishing Co., 1930. NYP

EDMONDS, Randolph. Shades and Shadows, (one act). In Shades
and Shadows, Edmonds, R. Boston: Meador Publishing Co., 1930.
NYP

EDMONDS, Randolph. Simon in Cyrene, 1939.

EDMONDS, Randolph. The Tribal Chief, (one act). In Shades and
Shadows, Edmonds, R. Boston: Meador Publishing Co., 1930. NYP

EDMONDS, Randolph. Wives and Blues, (unprod.), 1938.

EDMONDS, Randolph. Yellow Death, (one act), 1935. In The
Land of Cotton and Other Plays, Edmonds, R. Washington, D.C.:
Associated Publishers, Inc., 1943. NYP

EDWARDS, H.F.V. Job Hunters, (one act). In Crisis, Vol. 38, No. 12,
(December, 1931). NYP

ENGLAND, E. Angelo Herndon, 1936. New York: New Theatre League,
1935(?) Typescript. PAL

FERBER, Edna, and Kaufman, George. Stage Door, 1936. New York:
Dramatists Play Service, 1963. PAL

FINKLEHOFFE, Fred, and Monks, John. Brother Rat, 1936. New York:
Random House, 1937. NYP

FINN, Jonathan and Lawes, Warden. Chalked Out, 1937. In Best Plays of 1936-37, Mantle, Burns. PAL

FIRBANK, Ronald. Prancing Nigger, 193? FTP

FISHEL, H.L. Jericho, 193? FTP

FISHER, Rudolph. Conjur Man Dies, 1936. Typescript. Schom

FLAVIN, Martin. Achilles Had a Heel, 1935. New York: Samuel French, 1936. NYP

FLETCHER, Clinton, and Hurston, Zora, and Moore, Tim. Fast and Furious, (musical), 1931. In Best Plays of 1931-1932, Mantle, Burns. PAL

FORD, George, and Taylor, Ethel. Miss Gulliver Travels, 1931. In Best Plays of 1931-1932, Mantle, Burns. PAL

FOSTER, Norman, and Hamilton, Harry. Savage Rhythm, (musical), 1931. In Best Plays of 1931-32, Mantle, Burns. PAL

FRIEDMAN, Charles, and Rome, Harold. Sing Out the News, (musical), 1938. In Best Plays of 1938-1939, Mantle, Burns. PAL

FRIERSON, Annie. Quagmire, 193? FTP

FULLER, Lester. Babouk, 193? FTP

GEORGE, Charles. Way Down Upon the Swanee River. New York: Samuel French, 1930. NYP

GILBERT, Mercedes. Environment, (one act). In Selected Gems of Poetry, Comedy, and Drama. G. Mercedes. Boston: Christopher Publishing Co., 1931. NYP

GOLD, Michael and Blankfort, Michael. Battle Hymn, 1936. New York: Samuel French, 1936. FTP

GOLDSMITH, Clifford. What A Life, 1938. In Best Plays of 1937-1938, Mantle, Burns. PAL

GOODMAN, Arthur. If Booth Had Missed, 1932. New York: Samuel French, 1932. NYP

GOODRICH, Frances, and Hackett, Albert. Bridal Wise, 1932.

GOW, Ronald. John Brown, 1934.

GREEN, Eddie. Blackberries, (musical), 1932.

GREEN, Paul. Alma Mater, (one act). In One Act Plays for Stage
and Study. New York: Samuel French, 1938. NYP

GREEN, Paul. The House of Connelly, 1931. New York: Samuel French,
1931. NYP

GREEN, Paul. Hymn to the Rising Sun, (one act), 1936. Typescript.
FTP. PAL

GREEN, Paul. Potter's Field, 1931. In Out of the South. New York:
Harper & Bros., 1939. NYP

GREEN, Paul. Roll, Sweet Chariot (Potter's Field revised), 1934.
Typescript, PAL

GREEN, Paul. Shroud My Body Down. Iowa City: Clio Press, 1935.
NYP

GREEN, Paul. The Southern Cross, (one act). New York: Samuel
French, 1938. NYP

GREENSFELDER, Elmer. Swing Low, (one act). New York:
Longmans, Green & Co., 1934. NYP

GREGORY, Wayne. No Hidin' Place, (one act). San Francisco:
Banner Play Bureau, (pamphlets).

GROSS, Stephen, and Lait, Jack. The Hook-up, 1935. In Best
Plays of 1934-1935, Mantle, Burns. PAL

GUNNER, Frances. The Light of the Women, (pageant), 1930. In
Plays and Pageants from the Life of the Negro, Richardson, W.
(ed.). Washington, D.C.: Associated Publishers, 1930. NYP

HACKETT, Albert, and Goodrich, Frances. Bridal Wise, 1932.

HAILPARN, Dorothy. Horse Play, 1936. Typescript. FTP. PAL

HAMILTON, Harry, and Foster, Norman. Savage Rhythm, (musical),
1931. In Best Plays of 1931-1932, Mantle, Burns. PAL

HAMILTON, Roland. Crack of the Whip, 193? Columbus, Ohio:
Civic Theatre Guild, 193? Typescript. Schom

HARD, Parker. His Brother's Keeper, (one act). In The Yearbook of Short Plays, Series 2. Evanston, Ill.: Rowe Peterson, 1934. NYP

HARLOW, Ralph. It Might Have Happened in Alabama, (one act). In Crisis, 40:10, (Oct., 1933). NYP

HARRIS, Bernice. Judgement Comes to Dan'l, (one act), 1933. In Folk Plays of Eastern Carolina, Harris, Bernice (ed.). Chapel Hill: University Press, 1940. NYP

HARRIS, Helen Webb. Genefrede, (one act). In Negro History in Thirteen Plays, Richardson & Miller (eds.). Washington, D.C.: Associated Publishers, 1935. Schom

HART, Moss, and Berlin, Irving. Face the Music, (musical), 1932. In Best Plays of 1931-1932, Mantle, Burns. PAL

HART, Moss, and Kaufman, George. Once In A Lifetime, 1930. New York: Samuel French, 1933. NYP

HART, Moss, and Kaufman, George. You Can't Take It With You, 1937. New York: Dramatists Play Service, 1937. PAL

HAYES, Alfred, and Alexander, Leon. Journeyman, 1938. Typescript. PAL

HECHT, Ben, and MacArthur, Charles. Twentieth Century, 1932. SF

HELLMAN, Lillian. The Little Foxes, 1939. New York: Random House, 1939. NYP/DPS

HENDERSON, Ray, and Brown, Lew. Strike Me Pink, 1933. In Best Plays of 1932-1933, Mantle, Burns. PAL

HEYWARD, DuBose. Brass Ankle, 1931. New York: Farrar & Rinehart, 1931. NYP

HEYWARD, DuBose and Dorothy. Mamba's Daughters, 1939. New York: Farrar, 1939.

HEYWOOD, Donald. Africana, (operetta), 1934.

HEYWOOD, Donald. Black Rhythm, (musical), 1936. In Best Plays of 1936-1937, Mantle, Burns. PAL

HEYWOOD, Donald. How Come, Lawd?, 1937. In Best Plays of 1937-1938, Mantle, Burns. PAL

HEYWOOD, Donald. Ol'Man Satan, 1932. In Best Plays of 1932–1933, Mantle, Burns. PAL

HILL, Abram. Hell's Half Acre, 1938. Typescript. Schom

HILL, Abram, and Silvera, John. Liberty Deferred, (unprod.), 1936. Typescript. FTP. PAL

HILL, Abram. So Shall You Reap, (unprod.), 1938.

HILL Abram. Stealing Lightning, (one act), 1937.

HOLINER, Mann, and Dorfman, Nat, and Leslie, Lew. Blackbirds of 1933, (musical), 1933.

HOLM, John, and Abbott, George. Three Men on a Horse, 1935. New York: Dramatists Play Service, 1937. NYP

HOWARD, Garland, and Johnson, J.C. Change Your Luck, (musical), 1930. In Best Plays of 1929–1930, Mantle, Burns. PAL

HOWARD, Sidney. Yellow Jack, 1934. New York: Harcourt, Brace & Co., 1934. NYP

HUEY, Richard, and Moss, Carlton. Sacrifice, (one act), 1931.

HUGHES, Langston. Don't You Want to be Free?, (one act), 1938. In One Act Play Magazine II, (October, 1938). Schom

HUGHES, Langston. Joy to My Soul, 1937. Microfilm, 1963. Schom

HUGHES, Langston. Limitations of Life, (one act), 1938.

HUGHES, Langston. Little Eva's End, (one act), 1938.

HUGHES, Langston. Little Ham, 1935. In Five Plays by Langston Hughes, Smalley, Webster (ed.). Bloomington: Indiana University Press, 1968. PAL

HUGHES, Langston. Mulatto, 1935. In Five Plays by Langston Hughes, Smalley, Webster (ed.). Bloomington: Indiana University Press, 1968. PAL

HUGHES, Langston. Scottsboro Limited, (one act). In Four Poems and a Play in Verse. New York: Golden Stair, 1932. Schom

HUGHES, Langston. Soul Gone Home, (one act), 1937. In Five Plays by Langston Hughes, Smalley, Webster (ed.). Bloomington: Indiana University Press, 1968. PAL

HUGHES, Langston. St. Louis Woman, (unprod.), 1936. (Revision of Bontemps-Cullen script). Schom

HUGHES, Langston, and Still, William Grant. Troubled Island, 1936, (an opera version of Emperor of Haiti). New York: Leeds Music Corporation, 1949. PAL

HUGHES, Langston, and Bontemps, Arna. When The Jack Hollers. Microfilm, 1936. Schom

HULLEY, Lincoln. Suwanee River Jim. In Dramas in Twenty Volumes, VII, Hulley, L. (ed.). Deland, Fla.: E.O. Painter Co., 1933.

HURLBUT, Gladys. Ring Two, 1939. Typescript. PAL

HURLEY, Edward, and MacDonald, Ballard, and Morrisey, Will. Hot Rhythm, (musical), 1930.

HURSTON, Zora, and Fletcher, Clinton, and Moore, Tim. Fast and Furious, (musical), 1931. In Best Plays of 1931-1932, Mantle, Burns. PAL

HUSELL, Daniel. The Party's Over, 1933. In Best Plays of 1932-1933, Mantle, Burns. PAL

IDEN, Raymond. The Origin of Negro Minstrelsy and the Birth of Emmett's Dixie Land, (one act play with songs). Christian Music Publishing Co., 1938. Schom

JACKSON, William. Burning the Mortgage, (one act), 1931.

JACKSON, William. Four-Eleven, (one act), 1931(?).

JOHNSON, Georgia D. Frederick Douglass, (one act). In Negro History in Thirteen Plays, Richardson & Miller (eds.). Washington, D.C.: Associated Publishers, 1935. Schom

JOHNSON, Georgia. William and Ellen Craft, (one act). In Negro History in Thirteen Plays, Richardson & Miller (eds.). Washington, D.C.: Associated Publishers, 1935. Schom

JOHNSON, Hall. Run, Little Chillun, 1933. Typescript. Schom

JOHNSON, J.C., and Howard, Garland. Change Your Luck, (musical), 1930. In Best Plays of 1929-30, Mantle, Burns. PAL

JOHNSON, J.C. and Whipper, Leigh. Runnin' de Town, (musical), 1930.

KANDEL, Judith. Play, Genius, Play!, 1935. In Best Plays of 1935–1936, Mantle, Burns. PAL

KAUFMAN, George, and Hart, Moss. Once in a Lifetime, 1930. New York: Samuel French, 1933. NYP

KAUFMAN, George, and Ferber, Edna. Stage Door, 1936. New York: Dramatists Play Service, 1963. PAL

KAUFMAN, George, and Hart, Moss. You Can't Take It With You, 1937. New York: Dramatists Play Service, 1937. PAL

KAVANAUGH, Katherine. The Million Dollar Butler, 1933. Chicago: The Dramatic Publishing Co., 1933. NYP

KLINE, Herbert. John Henry. In New Theatre, (scenes only), (July, 1935.) PAL

LAIT, Jack, and Gross, Stephen. The Hook-Up, 1935. In Best Plays of 1934–1935, Mantle, Burns. PAL

LAMB, Arthur C. The Two Gifts, 1932. In Grinnell Plays, Chicago: The Dramatic Publishing Co., 1934. NYP

LANGNER, Lawrence, and Marshall, Armina. The Pursuit of Happiness, 1933. New York: Samuel French, 1934.

LAWES, Warden, and Finn, Johathan. Chalked Out, 1937. In Best Plays of 1936–37, Mantle, Burns. PAL

LAWSON, John Howard. Marching Song, 1937. In Best Plays of 1936–1937. Mantle, Burns. PAL

LESLIE, Lew. Blackbirds of 1939, (musical), 1939.

LESLIE, Lew, and Holiner, Mann, and Dorfman, Nat. Blackbirds of 1933, (musical), 1933.

LESLIE, Lew. Rhapsody in Black, (musical), 1931.

LEVY, Adolph. Go Down, Moses, (one act). In University of Michigan Plays, Rowe, Kenneth, (ed.). Ann Arbor, Michigan: George Wahr, 1932. NYP

LEWIS, Sinclair, and Lewis, Lloyd. Jayhawker, 1934. Garden City, N.Y.: Doubleday, Doran, & Co., Inc. 1935. NYP

LINK, Hannah, and Bennett, Dorothy. Woman's A Fool to be Clever, 1938. New York: Samuel French, 1939. NYP

LINK, Seymour G. Black Song, 193(?). FTP

LOOMIS, Clarence, and Newmeyer, Sarah. Susanna, Don't You Cry, (musical), 1939. Typescript. PAL

LYLES, Aubrey, and Miller, Flournoy. Lazy Rhythm, (musical), 1931.

MACARTHUR, Charles, and Hecht, Ben. Twentieth Century, 1932. SF

MCCARTHY, Mary. Please Mrs. Garibaldi, 1939. In Best Plays of 1938-1939, Mantle, Burns. PAL

MCCLENDON, Rose, and Bruce, Richard. Taxi Fare, (one act), 1931.

MACDONALD, Ballard, and Morrisey, Will, and Hurley, Edward. Hot Rhythm, (musical), 1930.

MCDONALD, Julian L. The Marriage of Cana, 1932.

MCENTEE, George. The Case of Philip Lawrence, 1937. Promptbook. PAL

MCGARTH, Frank. Carry Nation, 1932. In Best Plays of 1932-1933, Mantle, Burns. PAL

MCGEE, John. Jefferson Davis, 1936. In Best Plays of 1935-1936, Mantle, Burns. PAL

MCGOWAN, John. Singin' the Blues, 1931. In Best Plays of 1931-32, Mantle, Burns. PAL

MACK, Cecil, and Reddie, Milton. Swing It, (musical), 1937. FTP

MCNEIN, Denis. So Brave and So Free, 193? FTP

MACOWEN, Bernard, and Riewerts, J.P. The Blue Ghost, 1930. In Best Plays of 1929-1930, Mantle, Burns. PAL

MAIBAUM, Richard. Tree of Rope, 1932.

MANLEY, William F. Wild Waves, 1932. New York: Samuel French, 1932 NYP

MARSHALL, Armina, and Langner, Lawrence. The Pursuit of Happiness, 1933. New York: Samuel French, 1934.

MARTIN, Ted. Eviction, (one act), 1933(?).

MEYER, Annie N. Black Souls, 1932. Bedford, Mass.: Reynolds Press, 1932. NYP

MILLENS, James R. Never No More, 1932. In Best Plays of 1931-32, Mantle, Burns. PAL

MILLER, Allen C. The Opener of Doors, 193? FTP

MILLER, Flourney, and Razaf, Andy. Blackbirds of 1930, (musical), 1930.

MILLER, Flournoy, and Lyles, Aubrey. Lazy Rhythm, (musical), 1931.

MILLER, Flournoy, and Sissle, Noble. Shuffle Along of 1933, (musical), 1932.

MILLER, May. Christophe's Daughters, (one act). In Negro History in Thirteen Plays, Richardson & Miller (eds.). Washington, D.C.: Associated Publishers, 1935. Schom

MILLER, May. Graven Images, (one act), 1929. In Plays and Pageants from the Life of the Negro, Richardson, Willis (ed.). Washington, D.C.: Associated Publishers, 1930. Schom

MILLER, May. Harriet Tubman, (one act). In Negro History in Thirteen Plays, Richardson & Miller (ed.). Washington, D.C.: Associated Publishers, 1935. Schom

MILLER, May. Riding the Goat, (one act), 1929. Plays and Pageants from the Life of the Negro, Richardson & Miller (eds.). Washington, D.C.: Associated Publishers, 1930.

MILLER, May. Samory, (one act). In Negro History in Thirteen Plays, Richardson & Miller (eds.). Washington, D.C.: Associated Publishers, 1935. Schom

MILLER, May. Sojourner Truth, (one act). In Negro History in Thirteen Plays, Richardson & Miller (eds.). Washington, D.C.: Associated Publishers, 1935. Schom

MILLS, Billy, and Whipper, Leigh. Yeah Man, (musical), 1932.

MINTURN, Harry. The Swing Mikado, (musical), 1939. FTP

MONKS, John, and Finklehoffe, Fred. Brother Rat, 1936. New York: Random House, 1937. NYP

MOON, Llanon. Texas, the Land of the Strong. Austin, Texas: The Steck Company Publishers, 1936. NYP

MOORE, Tim, and Hurston, Zora, and Fletcher, Clinton. Fast and Furious, (musical), 1931. In Best Plays of 1931-1932, Mantle, Burns. PAL

MORELL, Peter, and Smith, J.A. Turpentine, 1936. FTP

MORRISEY, Will, and Hurley, Edward, and Macdonald, Ballard. Hot Rhythm, (musical), 1930.

MOSS, Carlton, and Huey, Richard. Sacrifice, (one act), 1931.

NEWMEYER, Sarah, and Loomis, Clarence. Susanna Don't You Cry, (musical), 1939. Typescript. PAL

NICHOLS, Anne, and Van Ronkel, Alfred. Pre-Honeymoon, 1936. In Best Plays of 1935-1936, Mantle, Burns. PAL

NIXON, Nora F. Cunjer Joe, (one act). New York: Samuel French, 1935. NYP

NORFORD, George. Joy Exceeding Glory, 1939. Typescript. Schom

NUTTER, Eileen. Humming Sam, (musical), 1933.

OBEY, Andre. Noah. London: Heineman Ltd., 1935. NYP

OLIVER, Richard, and Rimassa, John. Mess of Pottage, 1936. FTP

PATELSKY, Bella. Yo' Little Devil, (one act), 1934. In Seward Folio, (January 1934). Schom

PAWLEY, Thomas D. Freedom in My Soul, (one act), (unprod.), 1938.

PAWLEY, Thomas D. Jedgement Day, (one act), 1938. In The Negro Caravan. New York: Dryden Press, 1941.

PAWLEY, Thomas D. Smokey, (one act), 1939.

PAXTON, Dorothy. It's Better Fo' To Sing, 1939(?).

PAYTON, Lew. A Bitter Pill, (one act), 1937. In Did Adam Sin and Other Stories of Negro Life, Payton, L. Los Angeles: 1937. NYP

PAYTON, Lew. Chocolate Dandies in Bamville, (musical).

PAYTON, Lew. Did Adam Sin?, 1937. In Did Adam Sin and Other Stories of Negro Life, Payton, L. Los Angeles: 1937. NYP

PAYTON, Lew. A Flyin' Fool, (one act). In Did Adam Sin and Other Stories of Negro Life, Payton, L. Los Angeles: 1937. NYP

PAYTON, Lew. Some Sweet Day, (one act), 1937. In Did Adam Sin and Other Stories of Negro Life, Payton, L. Los Angeles: 1937. NYP

PAYTON, Lew. Two Sons of Ham, (one act). In Did Adam Sin and Other Stories of Negro Life, Payton, L. Los Angeles: 1937. NYP

PERKINS, Kenneth. Dance With Your Gods, 1934. Typescript. PAL

PERRY, Edward. Beauty Shop, (one act), 1930(?).

PETERKINS, Julia. Boy-Chillen, (one act). In One-Act Plays for Stage and Study: Seventh Series. New York: Samuel French, 1932. NYP

PETERKINS, Julia and Reed, Daniel. Scarlet Sister Mary, 1930. Typescript. PAL

PETERS, Paul, and Sklar, George. Bivouac.

PETERS, Paul and Sklar, George. Parade, 1936. Typescript. PAL

PETERS, Paul and Sklar, George. Stevedore, 1934. New York: Covici, Friede, 1934. NYP

PORTER, Washington. Return to Death, 193? FTP

PRATOR, Clifford. Dark Vallie, 1934.

PRATT, Theodore. The Big Blow, (musical), 1938. In Best Plays of 1938-1939, Mantle, Burns. PAL FTP

PRICE, Doris. The Bright Medallion, (one act). In University of Michigan Plays, Rowe, K. (ed.). Ann Arbor, Michigan: George Wahr, 1932. NYP

PRICE, Doris. The Eyes of the Old, (one act). In University of Michigan
Plays, Rowe, K. (ed.). Ann Arbor, Michigan: George Wahr, 1932.
NYP

PRICE, Doris. Two Gods, (one act). In Opportunity, X (Dec., 1932). NYP

PRIDE, Leo B. Fortune's Hired Man, (one act). In Shadow of the Mine.
New York, 193? FTP

RAINE, Norman, and Butler, Frank. Hangman's Whip, 1933. In
Best Plays of 1932-1933, Mantle, Burns. PAL

RANCH, Carty. The Mountain, 1933. Rock Island, Illinois: Frederick
Ingram, 1934. NYP

RAND, John. Murder at the DeSoto, (one act). New York: Samuel
French, 1938. NYP

RAPHAELSON, Samuel. White Man, 1936. In Accent on Youth and
White Man. New York: Samuel French, 1935. PAL

RAPP, William Jordan, and Thurman, Wallace. Jeremiah, The Magnificent,
1930(?). Typescript. Schom

RAZAF, Andy, and Miller, Flournoy. Blackbirds of 1930, (musical),
1930.

REDDIE, Milton, and Mack, Cecil. Swing It, (musical), 1937. FTP

REED, Daniel, and Peterkins, Julia. Scarlet Sister Mary, 1930.
Typescript. PAL

RICARDEL, Molly, and DuBois, William. I Love You Wednesday, 1932.
Typescript. PAL

RICE, Elmer. We, The People, 1933. Typescript. PAL

RICHARDSON, Thomas. Place: America. New York: NAACP,
1939. Schom

RICHARDSON, Willis. Antonio Maceo, (one act). In Negro History
in Thirteen Plays, Richardson & Miller (eds.). Washington, D.C.:
Associated Publishers, 1935. Schom

RICHARDSON, Willis. Attucks the Martyr, (one act). Negro History
in Thirteen Plays, Richardson & Miller, (eds.). Washington, D.C.:
Associated Publishers, 1935. Schom

RICHARDSON, Willis. The Broken Banjo, (revised). Typescript. Schom

RICHARDSON, Willis. The Dragon's Tooth, (one act). In The King's Dilemma and Other Plays for Children. New York: Exposition Press, 1956. Schom

RICHARDSON, Willis. The Elder Dumas, (one act). In Negro History in Thirteen Plays, Richardson & Miller (eds.). Washington, D.C.: Associated Publishers, 1935. Schom

RICHARDSON, Willis. In Menelik's Court, (one act), 1935. In Negro History in Thirteen Plays, Richardson & Miller, (eds.). Washington, D.C.: Associated Publishers, 1935. Schom

RICHARDSON, Willis. Near Calvary, (one act). In Negro History in Thirteen Plays, Richardson & Miller, (eds.). Washington, D.C.: Associated Publishers, 1935. Schom

RICHMAN, Carl. Brown Buddies, (musical), 1930. In Best Plays of 1930-1931, Mantle, Burns. PAL

RIEWERTS, J.P. and MacOwen, Bernard. The Blue Ghost, 1930. In Best Plays of 1929-1930, Mantle, Burns. PAL

RIMASSA, John and Oliver, Richard. Mess of Pottage, 1936. FTP

ROME, Harold, and Friedman, Charles. Sing Out the News, (musical), 1938. In Best Plays of 1938-1939, Mantle, Burns. PAL

ROSS, John M. One Clear Call. Nashville, Tenn.: Fisk University, 1936.

ROSS, John M. Rho Kappa Epsilon. Nashville, Tenn.: Fisk University, 1935.

ROSS, John M. Strivin', 1937.

SAROYAN, William. The Time of Your Life, 1939. New York: Samuel French, 1941.

SCHLICK, Frederick. Bloodstream, 1932. Boston: Walter Baker & Co., 1934.

SCHOENFELD, Bernard. Hitch Your Wagon, 1937. In Best Plays of 1936-1937, Mantle, Burns. PAL

SCHWARTZ, Arthur, and Dietz, Howard. At Home Abroad, (musical), 1935. In Best Plays of 1934-1935, Mantle, Burns. PAL

SEILER, Conrad. Sweet Land, 1937. FTP

SELDERS, Gilbert, and Charell, Eric. Swingin' The Dream, (musical), 1939. FTP

SELNICK, Eugene. The Gold Machine, (one act). In Drama Magazine, Vol. 20, No. 6, (March, 1930). PAL

SEYMOUR, Ann. Lawd, Does You Undahstan'?, (one act), 1936. In Representative One-Act Plays by American Authors, Mayorga, Margaret (ed.). Boston: Little, Brown & Co., 1937. PAL

SHERWOOD, Robert. Petrified Forest, 1935. New York: C. Scribner's Sons, 1935. NYP/DPS

SHIPMAN, Samuel, and Brown, Beth. Behind Red Lights, 1937.

SIEVERS, Wieder. Skin Deep, (one act). In The Carolina Magazine, (June, 1939).

SILVERA, Frank Alvin. Unto the Least, 1938. Typescript. Schom

SILVERA, John, and Hill, Abram. Liberty Deferred, (unprod.), 1936. Typescript. FTP. PAL

SISSLE, Noble, and Miller, Flournoy. Shuffle Along of 1933, (musical), 1932.

SKLAR, George, and Peters, Paul. Bivouac.

SKLAR, George, and Peters, Paul. Parade, 1935. Typescript. PAL

SKLAR, George, and Peters, Paul. Stevedore, 1934. New York: Covici, Friede, 1934. NYP

SMITH, J. Augustus. Louisiana, 1933. In Best Plays of 1932-1933, Mantle, Burns. PAL

SMITH, J. Augustus, and Morell, Peter. Turpentine, 1936. FTP

SPENCER, Raymond. Sex Hallelujah (Lysistrata), 193?. FTP

STALLINGS, Laurence, and Davis, Owen. Virginia, (musical), 1937. In Best Plays of 1937-1938, Mantle, Burns. PAL

STEIN, Gertrude. Four Saints in Three Acts, 1934. New York: Random House, 1934. NYP

STEINBECK, John. Of Mice and Men, 1937. New York: Covici, Friede, 1937. NYP/DPS

STEPHENS, Nan Bagby. The Green Vine, 1934. New York: Row, Peterson Co., 1934.

STOLLER, Maurice. We Are Men Again, 193? FTP

STREATOR, George. New Courage, (one act). In Crisis, Vol. 41, No. 1, (January, 1934). NYP

STURM, Justin. I Know What I Like, 1939. Typescript. PAL

TAYLOR, Ethel, and Ford, George. Miss Gulliver Travels, 1931. In Best Plays of 1931-1932, Mantle, Burns. PAL

TAZEWELL, Charles. Sugar Hill, (musical), 1931. In Best Plays of 1931-1932, Mantle, Burns. PAL

THOMAS, Albert E. Uncle Tom's Cabin. New York: D. Appleton-Century Co., 1934. NYP

THOMPSON, B.J. A Dixie Noon, (one act). In Normal Instructor, Vol. 39, (May, 1930).

THURMAN, Wallace, and Rapp, William Jordan. Jeremiah, The Magnificent, 1930(?). Typescript. Schom

TOTHEROH, Dan. Searching For The Sun, 1936. Typescript. PAL

TREADWELL, Sophie. Plumes in the Dust, 1936. Typescript. PAL

TRELLING, Ursala. Climbing Jacob's Ladder, (one act), 1931.

TYLER, Converse. White Heat, 193?. FTP

UNGER, Gladys. Noma, 1932.

VAN RONKEL, Alfred, and Nichols, Anne. Pre-Honeymoon, 1936.
In Best Plays of 1935-1936, Mantle, Burns. PAL

VOLLMER, Lulu. Sentinels, 1931. In Best Plays of 1931-1932, Mantle,
Burns. PAL

VOTEUR, Ferdinand. The Right Angle Triangle, 1939. In Best Plays
of 1938-1939, Mantle, Burns. PAL

WARD, Theodore. Big White Fog, 1937. Typescript. Schom

WARE, Alice H. Like A Flame. New York: New Theatre League, 1938.
NYP

WARE, Alice H. Mighty Wind A'Blowin', (one act), 1938. New York:
New Theatre League, 1936. NYP

WARE, Alice H. Together, (one act). In Theatre Workshop Magazine,
II (April-May-June, 1938).

WEBB, Kenneth. Zombie, 1932. In Best Plays of 1931-1932, Mantle,
Burns. PAL

WEITZENKORN, Louis. Five Star Final, 1930. New York: Samuel
French, 1931. NYP

WELLS, Frank. John Henry, 1936. Prompt Book. PAL

WEST, Mae. The Constant Sinner, 1931. In Best Plays of 1931-1932,
Mantle, Burns. PAL

WEXLEY, John. The Last Mile, 1930. New York: Samuel French, 1930.
NYP

WEXLEY, John. They Shall Not Die, 1934. New York: Knopf, 1934.
NYP

WHIPPER, Leigh, and Johnson, J.C. Runnin' de Town, (musical), 1930.

WHIPPER, Leigh, and Mills, Billy. Yeah Man, (musical), 1932.

WILBUR, Crane. The Monster, 1933.

WILDER, Robert. Sweet Chariot, 1930. In Best Plays of 1930-1931,
Mantle, Burns. PAL

WILSON, Frank. Brother Mose (Meek Mose revised), 1934. National
Service Bureau Publication #7. FTP. PAL

WILSON, Frank. Walk Together, Children, 1936. FTP

WOLFSON, Victor. Pastoral, 1939. Typescript. PAL

1940 - 1949

ARDREY, Robert. Jeb, 1945. In Plays of Three Decades, Ardrey, R.
New York: Atheneum, 1968. NYP

ANDERSON, Maxwell. Lost in the Stars, 1949. In Theatre Arts Magazine,
Vol. 34, (December, 1950).

ARCHIBALD, William. Carib Song, (musical), 1945.

BALZER, George, and Perrin, Sam. Are You With It, (musical), 1945.

BARKER, Albert, and Benson, Sally. Memphis Bound, (musical), 1945. In
Best Plays of 1944-1945, Mantle, Burns. PAL

BEHRMAN, Samuel N. The Pirate, 1942. New York: Random House,
1943. NYP

BENSON, Sally, and Barker, Albert. Memphis Bound, (musical), 1945.
In Best Plays of 1944-1945, Mantle, Burns. PAL

BLITZSTEIN, Marc. Regina, (musical), 1949.

BOLTON, Guy, and Levy, Parke, and Lipscott, Alan. Walk With Music,
(musical), 1940. In Best Plays of 1939-1940, Mantle, Burns. PAL

BONTEMPS, Arna, and Cullen, Countee. St. Louis Woman, 1946.
Typescript. Schom

BRADFORD, Roark. John Henry, 1940. New York: Harper & Bros.,
1939. Schom

BRONNER, Edwin. A Young American, 1946. Typescript. PAL

BROWN, Sonia. Strange Rain, (one act), 1945. In Best One Act Plays
of 1944, Mayorga, Margaret (ed.). New York: Dodd, Mead &
Co., 1945. NYP

BROWNE, Theodore. The Gravy Train, 1940. Typescript. Schom

BUTCHER, James W.,Jr. The Seer. In The Negro Caravan, Brown,
Sterling (ed.). New York: Dryden Press, Inc., 1941. NYP

CARROLL, Walter. Comin' For To Carry. In Twenty Prize Winning
Non-Royalty One-Act Plays, Smith, Betty (ed.). New York:
Greenberg, 1943. PAL

CARROLL, Walter. Culcha, (one act). In Twenty-five Non-Royalty
One-Act Plays for All Girl Casts, Smith, Betty (ed.). New York:
Greenberg, 1942. PAL

CARROLL, Walter. De Lost John. In Carolina Playbook, Vol. 15.
Chapel Hill: University Press, 1942.

CARROLL, Walter, and Goodman, Randolph. A Long Way from Home,
1948. Typescript. PAL

CARROLL, Walter. Tin Top Valley, 1947. ANT

CHODOROV, Edward. Decision, 1944. Typescript. PAL

CLEMENTS, Colin, and Ryerson, Florence. Harriet, 1943. New York:
Samuel French, 1945. NYP

COLEMAN, William Lawrence. Wreath Without Laurel, (one act),
1940. Alabama University Blackfriars Series of Original Plays,
No. 4. PAL

COLEMAN, William Lawrence. ---I Cat Hattie and Kingdom Come, 1942.
Alabama University Blackfriars Series of Original Plays, No. 52.
PAL

CONKLE, Ellsworth P. According to Law, (one act), 1940.

COOKSEY, Curtis. Starlight, 1942. Typescript. ANT PAL

COOPER, Lew. Run Little Chillun, 194? Typescript. Schom

CRAWFORD, Myrtle. Negro Builds a Pyramid, (pageant). In
Social Studies, 32, (January, 1941).

CULLEN, Countee, and Dodson, Owen. The Third Fourth of July, (one act).
   In Theatre Arts Magazine, Vol. 30, (1946). PAL

CULLEN. Countee and Arna, Bontemps. St. Louis Woman, 1946. Typescript.
   Schom.

DAVIS, Leslie, and Harton, Margaret. Night Life of a Teacher, 1940.
   In Alabama University Blackfriars Series of Original Plays, No.
   6, Raines, Lester (ed.). PAL

DAVIS, Ossie. Alexis is Fallen, (unprod.), 1947.

DAVIS, Ossie. The Mayor of Harlem (unprod.), 1949.

DAVIS, Ossie. Point Blank, (unprod.), 1949.

DAVIS, Ossie. They Seek A City, (unprod.), 1947.

DEMPSEY, David. It Ain't Brooklyn, (one act). In Best One Act Plays of
   1944, Mayorga, Margaret (ed.). New York: Dodd, Mead, & Co.,
   1945. NYP

DODSON, Owen. The Ballad of Dorie Miller, (one act), 1942. Manuscript.
   YL

DODSON, Owen. Bayou Legend, 1946.

DODSON, Owen. Doomsday Tale, 1941(?). Manuscript. YL

DODSON, Owen. Everybody Join Hands, (one act), 1942. In
   Theatre Arts Magazine, Vol. 27. PAL

DODSON, Owen. Freedom the Banner, 1942. Manuscript. YL

DODSON, Owen. New World A Coming, (pageant), 1944(?). Typescript.
   Schom

DODSON, Owen. The Southern Star, (unprod.), 1940. Manuscript. YL

DODSON, Owen, and Cullen, Countee. The Third Fourth of July,
   (one act), 1945. In Theatre Arts Magazine, Vol. 30, (1946).

DUNNE, George H. Trial By Fire, 1947.

D'USSEAU, Arnaud and Gow, James. Deep Are the Roots, 1946. New York:
   Dramatists Play Service, 1946. PAL

EASTMAN, Fred. American Saint of Democracy, (one act), 1942. In
Plays of Democracy, Mayorga, M. (ed.). New York: Dodd,
Mead & Co., 1944. PAL

EDMONDS, Randolph. Earth and Stars, 1946.

EDMONDS, Randolph. G.I. Rhapsode, 1943.

EDMONDS, Randolph. The Land of Cotton, 1942(?). In The Land
of Cotton and Other Plays, Edmonds, R. Washington, D.C.:
Associated Publishers, Inc., 1943. NYP

EDMONDS, Randolph. The Shadow Across the Path, (one act),
(unprod.), 1943.

EDMONDS, Randolph. The Shape of Wars to Come, (one act), 1943.

EDMONDS, Randolph. The Trial and Banishment of Uncle Tom,
(one act), 1945.

ELISCU, Edward. "The Same Old South" in Meet The People, (musical),
1940. In Best Plays of 1940-1941, Mantle, Burns. PAL

FRANKEN, Rose. Outrageous Fortune, 1943. Typescript, 1943. PAL

GOODMAN, Randolph and Carroll, Walter. A Long Way From Home,
1948. Typescript. PAL

GRAHAM, Shirley. Dust to Earth, 1940.

GRAHAM, Shirley. I Gotta Home, 1942.

GRAVES, Clifford. Not Unto Us, 1940. Typescript. Schom

GREEN, Paul, and Wright, Richard. Native Son, 1941. New York:
Harper & Bros., 1941. NYP/SF

HAMMERSTEIN, Oscar. Carmen Jones, 1943. New York: Knopf, 1945.

HAMMERSTEIN, Oscar and Rodgers, Richard. South Pacific, 1949. New
York: Random House, 1949.

HARBURG, E.Y. and Saidy, Fred. Finian's Rainbow, 1947. New York:
Random House, 1947.

HARTON, Margaret. Blessed Be The Bride, (one act), 1942. In
Alabama University Blackfriar Series of Original Plays, No. 43,
Raines, Lester (ed.). PAL

HARTON, Margaret, and Davis, Leslie. Night Life of a Teacher, 1940. In Alabama University Blackfriars Series of Original Plays, No. 6, Raines, Lester (ed.). PAL

HELLMAN, Lillian. Another Part of the Forest, 1946. Typescript. PAL/DPS

HELLMAN, Lillian. The Searching Wind, 1944. Typescript, 1944. PAL

HEYWARD, Dorothy. New Georgia, 1944. Typescript. Schom

HEYWARD, Dorothy. Set My People Free, 1948. Typescript. PAL

HEYWARD, Dorothy, and Rigsby, Howard. South Pacific, 1943. Typescript. PAL

HILL, Abram. Power of Darkness, 1948.

HILL, Abram. On Striver's Row, 1940. Typescript. ANT Schom

HILL, Abram. Walk Hard, 1944. Typescript. ANT PAL

HOLLIFIELD, Harold. Cow in the Apartment, 194?

HOUSTON, Noel. According to Law, (one act), 1940. In One Act Play Magazine, Vol. 3, (1940). NYP

HUGHES, Langston. For This We Fight, 194? YL

HUGHES, Langston, and Rice, Elmer. Street Scene, (folk opera), 1947.

HUGHES, Langston. The Sun Do Move; A Music Play, 1942. Mimeograph. Schom

HUNTER, Eddie, and Sweeting, Earle. The Lady, 194? Typescript. Schom

HURSTON, Zora Neale, and Waring, Dorothy. Polk County, A Comedy of Negro Life on a Sawmill Camp, 1944. Typescript. PAL

JOHNSON, James J. and Miller, Flournoy. Meet Miss Jones, (musical), 1947.

KINGSLEY, Sidney. Detective Story, 1949. New York: Dramatists Play Service, 1951. PAL

KINGSLEY, Sidney and Madge. The Patriots, 1943. New York: Random House, 1943.

KOMAI, Felicia. Cry, The Beloved Country. New York: Friendship Press, 1955. NYP

KRONTZ, Samuel. Home Is The Hunter, 1945.

KULLER, Sid, and Ellington, Duke. Jump For Joy, (musical), 1941.

LAMB, Arthur C. Black Woman in White, 1941.

LA TOUCHE, John. Beggar's Holiday, 1946. Typescript. PAL

LAURENTS, Arthur. Home of the Brave, 1946. New York: Random House, 1946. NYP

LEE, Harry. A Nickel Whistle, 1946. Typescript. Schom

LEONTOVICH, Eugenie and Miramova, Elena. Dark Eyes, 1943. New York: Dramatists Play Service, 1943.

LERNER, Alan J. Love Life, (musical), 1948.

LEVY, Parke, and Lipscott, Alan, and Bolton, Guy. Walk With Music, (musical), 1940. In Best Plays of 1939-1940, Mantle, Burns. PAL

LEWIS, Kate. The Scarlet Petticoat, (one act), 1940. In Alabama Folk Plays, Lewis, Kate (ed.). Chapel Hill: University Press, 1943. NYP

LEWIS, Kate. Three Links o' Chain, (one act), 1940. In Alabama Folk Plays, Lewis, Kate. Chapel Hill: University Press, 1943. NYP

LEWIS, Kate. Watermelon Time, (one act), 1940. In Alabama Folk Plays, Lewis, Kate. Chapel Hill: University Press, 1943. NYP

LICHTY, Justin. Mississippi Moon, 1943(?). Typescript. Schom

LIPSCOTT, Alan, and Bolton, Guy, and Levy, Parke. Walk With Music, (musical), 1940. In Best Plays of 1939-1940, Mantle, Burns. PAL

LOOS, Anita. Happy Birthday, 1945. New York: Samuel French, 1948. NYP

MCGLYNN, Rev. Thomas. Caukey, 1943.

MARION, George Jr. and Waller, T.W. Early to Bed, (musical), 1943. In Best Plays of 1943-1944, Mantle, Burns. PAL

MEISER, Edith. The Strangler Fig, 1940. In Best Plays of 1939-1940, Mantle, Burns. PAL

MILLER, Flournoy and Johnson, James J. Meet Miss Jones, (musical), 1947.

MILLER, Toby. Johnny Noble, 1946. Typescript. PAL

MIRAMOVA, Elena, and Leontovich, Eugenie. Dark Eyes, 1943. New York: Dramatists Play Service, 1943.

MITCHELL, Loften. The Bancroft Dynasty, 1948.

NAGLE, Urban. City of Kings, 1949. New York: Christopher Press, 1949. NYP

NUGENT, Elliott, and Thurber, James. The Male Animal, 1940. New York: Random House, 1940. NYP/SF

ODETS, Clifford. The Big Knife, 1949. New York: Random House, 1949. PAL/DPS

O'NEILL, Eugene. The Iceman Cometh, 1946. New York: Random House, 1946. NYP

OSCAR, Saul, and Mays, H.R. Medicine Show, (musical), 1940. In Best Plays of 1939-1940, Mantle, Burns. FTP PAL

PAWLEY, Thomas D. Crispus Attucks, 1947.

PAWLEY, Thomas D. Messiah, (eight scenes), 1948.

PAWLEY, Thomas D. Zebedee, (unprod.), 1949.

PERRIN, Sam and Balzer, George. Are You With It, (musical), 1945.

PYZEL, Robert. Anybody Home, 1949.

REGAN, Sylvia. Morning Star, 1940. New York: Dramatists Play Service, 1940. NYP

REINES, Bernard. Forward the Heart, 1949. Typescript. PAL

RICE, Elmer, and Hughes, Langston. Street Scene, (folk opera), 1947. SF

RICE, Elmer. Two on an Island, 1940. New York: Coward-McCann, Inc., 1940. NYP

RICHARDS, Stanley. District of Columbia, (one act). In Opportunity, (April-June 1945).

RICHARDSON, Willis. Miss or Mrs., (one act), 1941.

ROBINSON, Valerie. Casper Holstein, 1947.

ROGERS, Merrill. Book of Job, (one act). In One Act Plays for Stage and Study, 10th Series. New York: Samuel French, 1949. PAL

RODGERS, Richard and Hammerstein, Oscar. South Pacific, 1949. New York: Random House, 1949.

ROOT, Lynn. Cabin In The Sky, 1949. Typescript. PAL

ROSS, John M. The Sword, 1948.

RUDLEY, Barett and Herbert. How Long Til Summer, 1949.

RYERSON, Florence, and Clements, Colin. Harriet, 1943. New York: Samuel French, 1945. NYP

SAIDY, Fred, and Harburg, E. Y. Finian's Rainbow, 1947. New York: Random House, 1947.

SAROYAN, William. Across the Board on Tomorrow Morning, (one act). New York: Harcourt, Brace & Co., 1941.

SARTRE, Jean-Paul. The Respectful Prostitute, (one act), 1946. In No Exit and Three Other Plays. New York: Vintage Paper, 1946. PAL

SHERMAN, Nat. The Washington Years, 1947.

SHULL, Leo. What's Your Epitaph?, 194? Typescript. Schom

SMITH, Lillian and Esther. Strange Fruit, 1945. Typescript. PAL

SPEWACK, Samuel. Two Blind Mice, 1949. New York: Dramatists Play Service, 1949.

STEELE, Owen. Trouble in July, 1949.

STEPHENS, Nan B. Lily. New York: Row, Peterson & Co., 1940.

STEWART, Donald Ogden. How I Wonder, 1947.

SWEETING, Earle, and Hunter, Eddie. The Lady, 194? Typescript.
Schom

THURBER, James, and Nugent, Elliott. The Male Animal, 1940.
New York: Random House, 1940. NYP/SF

TURNEY, Robert. The Secret Room, 1945. Typescript. PAL

TUTT, J. Homer. De Gospel Train (Jim Crow), 1940. Typescript.
Schom

UNKELBACH, Kurt. The Peacemaker, 1946. ANT

VAN DRUTEN, John. Old Acquaintance, 1940. Typescript. PAL

WALLER, T.W. and Marion, George Jr. Early to Bed, (musical), 1943.
In Best Plays of 1943-1944, Mantle, Burns. PAL

WARD, Theodore. Our Lan', 1946. In A Theatre in Your Head, Rowe,
Kenneth, (ed.). New York: Funk and Wagnall, 1960. PAL

WARING, Dorothy, and Hurston, Zora Neale. Polk County, A Comedy of
Negro Life on a Sawmill Camp, 1944. Typescript. PAL

WEBER, Margaret H. George Washington Fourth, (one act). Evanston,
Ill.: Row, Peterson, & Co., 1942. NYP

WHITE, Kenneth. Freight, (one act), 1946. In The Best One-Act
Plays of 1946-1947, Mayorga, M. (ed.). New York: Dodd,
Mead & Co., 1947. PAL

WILDER, Robert and Sally. Flamingo Road, 1945. Typescript. PAL

WILLIAMS, Tennessee. Streetcar Named Desire. Connecticut:
New Directions, 1947. NYP/DPS

WOOD, Maxine. On Whitman Avenue, 1946. New York: Dramatists
Play Service, 1948. NYP

WRIGHT, Richard and Green, Paul. Native Son, 1941. New York:
Harper & Bros., 1941. NYP

YORDAN, Philip. Anna Lucasta, 1944. New York: Dramatists Play
Service, 1950. NYP

ADDINSELL, Richard and Dane, Clemence. Come of Age, 1952.
Garden City, New York: Doubleday, Doran & Co. Inc.,
1934. LC

AKAR, John J. Valley Without Echo, 1957.

ALEXANDER, Frank and Krumschmidt, E.A. The Gentle Folks, 1952.

ANONYMOUS. Ride the Right Bus, 1951.

ANONYMOUS. South of Atlanta, (one act), 1957.

APPLEGARTH, Margaret T. Were You There? In Four Playettes,
Applegarth, Daily, and Wolfe. New York: Friendship Press,
1956.

BENSON, Sally. Seventeen, (musical), 1951. In Best Plays of 1951-1952,
Chapman, John. PAL

BILOWIT, Ira and Lehr, Wilson. Of Mice and Men, (musical), 1958.

BRANCH, William. Baccalaureate, (unprod.), 1954. Typescript. PAL

BRANCH, William. In Splendid Error, 1953. Typescript. Schom

BRANCH, William. Light in the Southern Sky, (one act), 1958.

BRANCH, William. A Medal for Willie, 1951. Typescript. Schom

CAPOTE, Truman. The Grass Harp, 1952. New York: Dramatists Play
Service, 1954. PAL
CAPOTE, Truman. The House of Flowers, 1954. New York: Random
House, 1968. PAL

CHILDRESS, Alice. Florence, (one act). In Masses and Mainstream, Vol.
III, (October, 1950). NYP

CHILDRESS, Alice. Gold Through the Trees, 1952.

CHILDRESS, Alice. Just a Little Simple, 1950.

CHILDRESS, Alice. A Man Bearing A Pitcher.

CHILDRESS, Alice. Trouble in Mind, 1955.

CHILDRESS, Alice. Wedding Band.

CHODOROV, Jerome and Fields, Joseph. The Ponder Heart, 1956.
New York: Random House, 1954. PAL

COLEMAN, Lonnie. Jolly's Progress, 1959. In Best Plays of 1959-1960,
Kronenberger, Louis. PAL

COOPER, Norton. The Ballad of Jazz Street, 1959.

CORWIN, Norman. The Rivalry, 1959. New York: Dramatists Play
Service, 1960. NYP

CROUSE, Russell and Lindsay, Howard. Remains To Be Seen, 1951. New
York: Random House, 1951. NYP

CRUMP, Owen. Southern Exposure, 1950. New York: Dramatists Play
Service, 1951. PAL

DACOSTA, Morton. Saratoga, 1959. Typescript, 1959. PAL

DANE, Clemence and Addinsell, Richard. Come of Age, 1952.
Garden City, New York: Doubleday Doran & Co., Inc., 1934.
LC

DARION, Joe. Shinbone Alley, 1957. Typescript, 1957. PAL

DAVIS, Eddie and Bolton, Guy. Ankles Aweigh, (musical), 1954.

DAVIS, Ossie. Alice in Wonder, (one act), 1953.

DAVIS, Ossie. The Big Deal, 1953.

DAVIS, Ossie. Clay's Rebellion, (unprod.), 1951.

DAVIS, Ossie. Montgomery Footprints, (one act), 1956.

DEVANY, Edward. The Cow-Catcher on the Caboose, (one act), 1959.
In Best Short Plays of 1958-1959, Mayorga, Margaret (ed.).
Boston: Beacon Press, 1959. PAL

DINELLI, Mel. The Man. New York: Dramatists Play Service, 1950.

DODSON, Owen. The Christmas Miracle, (one act, musical), 1955.

DRAYTON, Mary. Debut, 1953. Typescript. PAL

DREW, B., and Hughes, Langston, and Mann, Abby. Just Around the Corner,
(musical), 1951. Typescript. Schom

EASTON, Sidney. Miss Trudie Fair, 195?

EATON, James. Color Scheme, 1957.

EDMONDS, Randolph. Career or College (A Purpose Play), (one act), 1956.

EDMONDS, Randolph. Prometheus and the Atom, 1955.

EDMONDS, Randolph. Whatever the Battle Be (A Symphonic Drama), 1950.

FAULKNER, William, and Ford, Ruth. Requiem for a Nun, 1959. New York: Random House, 1959. NYP

FIELDS, Dorothy & Herbert, and Mamoulian, Rouben. Arms and the Girl, (musical), 1950. Typescript. PAL

FIELDS, Dorothy, and Schwartz, Arthur. By the Beautiful Sea, (musical), 1954. Typescript, 1954. PAL

FIELDS, Joseph, and Chodorov, Jerome. Anniversary Waltz, 1954. New York: Random House, 1954. PAL

FIELDS, Joseph, and Chodorov, Jerome. The Ponder Heart, 1956. New York: Random House, 1954. PAL

FORD, Ruth, and Faulkner, William. Requiem for a Nun, 1959. New York: Random House, 1959.

FRIEDMAN, Charles. My Darlin' Aida, (musical), 1952. In Best Plays of 1951-52, Chapman, John. PAL

FULLER, Lorenzo, and Mills, Carley. The World's My Oyster, 1956(?).

FURMAN, Roger. Fool's Paradise, (one act), 1952.

FURMAN, Roger. The Quiet Laughter, (one act), 1952.

GAZZA, Michael. A Hatful of Rain, 1955. Typescript. PAL

GELBER, Jack. The Connection, 1959. New York: Grove Press,
1960. NYP

GELLER, Bruce, and Wasserman, Dale. Livin' the Life, (musical),
1957. Typescript, 1957. PAL

GIBSON, William. The Miracle Worker, 1959. New York:
Samuel French, 1960. PAL

GLENN, Robert, and Hughes, Langston. Shakespeare in
Harlem, 1959.

GLICKMAN, Will, and Stein, Joseph. The Body Beautiful,
(musical), 1958. New York: Samuel French, 1957. PAL

GLICKMAN, William, and Stein, Joseph. Mr. Wonderful, (musical),
1956. Typescript. PAL

GREEN, Paul. The Confederacy. New York: Samuel French, 1959.
NYP

GREEN, Paul. Fine Wagon. In Wings for to Fly. New York:
Samuel French, 1959. NYP

GREEN, Paul. Lay This Body Down. In Wings for to Fly. New
York: Samuel French, 1959. NYP

GREEN, Paul. The Thirsting Heart. In Wings for to Fly. New
York: Samuel French, 1959. NYP

GREEN, Paul. Wilderness Road, 1955. New York: Samuel French,
1956. NYP

HANSBERRY, Lorraine. Raisin in the Sun, 1959. New York:
Samuel French, 1959.

HARBURG, E.Y. and Saidy, Fred. Jamaica, (musical), 1957.

HARRIS, Tom. The A Number One Family, (one act), (unprod.), 1958.

HARRIS, Tom. The Dark Years, (one act), (unprod.), 1958.

HARRIS, Tom. Fall of an Iron Horse, 1959. U.C.L. A.: Master's Thesis Play, 1959.

HARRIS, Tom. Pray for Daniel Adams, (one act), 1958.

HARRIS, Tom. Woman in the House, (one act), (unprod.), 1958.

HART, Moss. The Climate of Eden, 1952. Typescript. PAL/DPS

HEALEY, Robert M. Nobody Knows. Boston: Bakers Plays, 1958.

HELLMAN, Lillian. The Autumn Garden, 1951. Boston: Little, Brown, 1951. NYP

HERBERT, Frederick H. A Girl Can Tell, 1953. Typescript. PAL

HILL, Abram. Miss Mabel, (unprod.), 1951.

HOLLIFIELD, Harold. J. Troth, 195?

HOWARD, Sally. The Jackal, 195?

HUGHES, Langston. Simple Takes a Wife; a Negro Folk Comedy. "The original dramatic version of the novel". Typescript, 195? Schom

HUGHES, Langston, and Glenn, Robert. Shakespeare in Harlem, 1959.

HUGHES, Langston, and Mann, Abby, and Drew, B. Just Around the Corner, (musical), 1951. Typescript. Schom

HUGHES, Langston, and Martin, David (music). Simply Heavenly, (musical), 1957. In Five Plays by Langston Hughes, Smalley, Webster (ed.). Bloomington: Indiana University Press, 1968. PAL

HUGHES, Langston, and Meyerowitz, Jan. The Barrier (a musical version of Hughes' Mulatto), 1950. Typescript.

JEANETTE, Gertrude. A Bolt from the Blue, 1952.

JEANETTE, Gertrude. This Way Forward, 1951.

JOHNSON, Greer, and Sebree, Charles. Mrs. Patterson, 1954. In
   Best Plays of 1954-1955, Hewes, Henry. PAL

JOHNSON, J. C. The Year Around, (musical), 1953.

KAUFMAN, George S. and McGrath, Leveen. Fancy Meeting You Again,
   1952. New York: Dramatists Play Service, 1951. NYP

KAUFMAN, George S. and McGrath, Leveen. The Small Hours, 1951.
   New York: Dramatists Play Service, 1951. NYP

KAZAN, Molly. The Egghead, 1957. New York: Dramatists
   Play Service, 1958. PAL

KERR, Jean. King of Hearts, 1954. Garden City: Doubleday, 1954.
   NYP

KESSELRING, Joseph. Four Twelves Are Forty Eight, 1951. New York:
   Dramatists Play Service, 1951. NYP

KIRKLAND, Jack. The Man With the Golden Arm, 1955.

KRAMM, Joseph. The Shrike, 1952. New York: Random House, 1952. NYP

KRUMSCHMIDT, E.A. and Alexander, Frank. The Gentle Folks, 1952.

LAKE, Goldie. Glory Day, (one act), 1951. In Best One-Act Plays of
   1951-1952, Mayorga, Margaret (ed.). New York: Dodd Mead & Co.,
   1952. NYP

LAMB, A. Clifton. Roughshod Up the Mountain, 1956.

LA TOUCHE, John, and Lights, Frederick. Samson and Lila Dee,
   (musical), 1953.

LAWRENCE, Jerome, & Lee, Robert. Only in America, 1959. New York:
   Samuel French, 1960. PAL

LAWRENCE, Reginald and Taylor, Dwight. Out of This World,
   (musical), 1950.

LEE, Robert, & Lawrence, Jerome. Only in America, 1959. New York:
   Samuel French, 1960. PAL

LEHER, Wilson, and Bilowit, Ira. Of Mice and Men, (musical), 1958.

LENSKI, Lois. The Bean-Pickers, (one act). New York: National Council of Churches, 1952.

LEVIN, Ira. Interlock, 1958. New York: Dramatists Play Service, 1958. PAL

LEVIN, Ira. No Time For Sergeants, 1955. New York: Dramatists Play Service, 1958. PAL

LIBOTT, Robert and Paton, Alan. Too Late the Phalarope, 1956. Typescript, 1956. PAL

LIGHTS, Frederick, and La Touche, John. Samson and Lila Dee, (musical), 1953.

LINDSAY, Howard and Crouse, Russel. Remains to be Seen, 1951. New York: Random House, 1951. NYP/DPS

LOGAN, Joshua. Wisteria Trees, 1950. New York: Random House, 1958. NYP/DPS

MAAT, Jan. The South Wind Blows North. New York: William-Frederick Press, 1958. NYP

MCBROWN, Gertrude P. Birthday Surprise, (one act). In Negro History Bulletin, Vol. XVI, No. 5, (February, 1953). NYP

MCCULLERS, Carson. The Member of the Wedding, 1950. New York: New Directions, 1951. NYP/DPS

MCGRATH, Leveen and Kaufman, George S. The Small Hours, 1951. New York: Dramatists Play Service, 1951. NYP

MCGRATH, Leveen and Kaufman, George S. Fancy Meeting You Again, 1952. New York: Dramatists Play Service, 1951. NYP

MAMOULIAN, Rouben, and Fields, Dorothy and Herbert. Arms and the Girl, (musical), 1950. PAL

MANN, Abby, and Drew, B., and Hughes, Langston. Just Around the Corner, (musical), 1951. Typescript. Schom

MARCHANT, William. The Desk Set, 1955. New York: Samuel French, 1956. PAL

MAYFIELD, Julian. The Other Foot, (one act), 1952.

MAYFIELD, Julian. A World Full of Men, (one act), 1952.

MILLER, Arthur. The Crucible, 1953. New York: The Viking Press, 1953.
PAL

MILLER, Clifford L. Wings Over Dark Waters. New York: Great-Concord
Publishers, 1954.

MILLS, Carley, and Fuller, Lorenzo. The World's My Oyster, 1956(?).

MITCHELL, Loften. The Cellar, 1952.

MITCHELL, Loften. Land Beyond the River, 1957. Cody, Wyo.:
Pioneer Drama Service, 1963. Schom

NORFORD, George. Head of the Family, 1950.

OGDEN, Jean. Country Gentleman. New York: Exposition Press, 1950.

PANETTA, George. Comic Strip, 1958. New York: Samuel French,
1958. PAL

PARKER, John W. Sleep on, Lemuel, (one act). In North Carolina Drama,
Walser, Richard (ed.). Richmond: Garrett and Massie, 1956. NYP

PATON, Alan, and Libott, Robert. Too Late the Phalarope, 1956. Typescript,
1956. PAL

PATRICK, John. The Hasty Heart, 1945. New York: Dramatists Play
Service, 1945.

PETERS, Paul. Nat Turner, 1950. In Cross-Section, Seaver, Edwin
(ed.). New York: L.B. Fischer, 1944. Schom

PETERSON, Lewis. Take A Giant Step, 1953. New York: Samuel French,
1954. NYP

PINES, Les. The Fishermen, 1954.

POLLACK, Ed. Wedding in Japan, 1957.

RAPHLING, Sam. Carry Me Back (The Story of James Bland),
(one act opera), 1957.

REAVIN, Sara. The Ivory Branch, 1956.

RELLA, Ettore. Sign of Winter, 1958.

RICE, Elmer. The Winner, 1954. New York: Dramatists Play Service, 1954. PAL

RICHARDSON, Willis. The Gypsy's Finger Ring, (one act). In The King's Dilemma and Other Plays for Children. New York: Exposition Press, 1956. Schom

RICHARDSON, Willis. Man of Magic, (one act). In The King's Dilemma and Other Plays for Children. New York: Exposition Press, 1956. Schom

RICHARDSON, Willis. The New Santa Claus, (one act). In The King's Dilemma and Other Plays for Children. New York: Exposition Press, 1956. Schom

ROBINSON, Earl and Waldo, Salt. Sandhog, (musical), 1954. Typescript. PAL

ROBINSON, William. The Anger of One Young Man, 1959.

ROBINSON, William. The Passing Grade, 1958.

ROME, Harold. Bless You All, (musical), 1950.

ROSS, John M. Wanga Doll. New Orleans, La.: Dillard University, 1954.

ROSTEN, Norman. Mr. Johnson, 1956. New York: Dramatists Play Service, 1969.

RUBIN, Barnard. The Candy Store, 1951.

SAIDY, Fred, and Harburg, E. Y. Jamaica, (musical), 1957.

SALT, Waldo, and Robinson, Earl. Sandhog, (musical), 1954. Typescript. PAL

SAWYER, Robert Earl. A Race with the Wind, 1958.

SCHARY, Dore. Sunrise at Campobello, 1958. New York: Dramatists Play Service, 1961. PAL

SCHULMAN, Arnold. A Hole in the Head, 1957. New York: Samuel French, 1957. PAL

SCHWARTZ, Arthur & Fields, Dorothy. By the Beautiful Sea, (musical), 1954. Typescript, 1954. PAL

SEBREE, Charles, and Johnson, Greer. Mrs. Patterson, 1954. In Best Plays of 1954-1955, Hewes, Henry. PAL

SERGEL, Christopher. Winesburg, Ohio, 1958. In Best Plays of 1957-1958, Kronenberger, Louis. PAL

SHERWOOD, Robert. Small War on Murray Hill, 1957. New York: Dramatists Play Service, 1957. PAL

SHIFFRIN, A.B. Angel in the Pawnshop, 1951. New York: Dramatists Play Service, 1951. NYP

SHINE, Ted. The Bats Out of Hell, (unprod.), 1955.

SHINE, Ted. Cold Day in August, (one act), 1950.

SHINE, Ted. Dry August, (unprod.), 1952.

SHINE, Ted. Entourage Royale, (musical), (unprod.), 1958.

SHINE, Ted. Epitaph for a Bluebird, 1958.

SHINE, Ted. A Rat's Revolt, (unprod.), 1959.

SHINE, Ted. Sho' Is Hot in the Cotton Patch, (one act), 1951. In Encore Magazine, Vol. XI. Tallahassee, Florida: Florida A&M University, (1967). Produced NEC, 1968 under title Miss Weaver.

SINCLAIR, Jo. The Long Moment, 1950.

SOMMER, Edith. A Roomful of Roses, 1955. New York: Dramatists Play Service, 1956. PAL

STAVIS, Barrie. Banners of Steel, 1951. Typescript. PAL

STAVIS, Barrie. The Man Who Never Died, 1954. New York: Dramatists Play Service, 1959.

STEIN, Joseph & Glickman, William. The Body Beautiful, (musical), 1958. New York: Samuel French, 1957.

STEIN, Joseph, and Glickman, William. Mr. Wonderful, (musical), 1956. Typescript. PAL

STEIN, Sol. A Shadow of My Enemy, 1957. Typescript, 1957. PAL

STRADLEY, John. Alley of the Sunset, 1959.

STUCKY, William. Touchstone, 1953. Typescript. PAL

SWANN, Darius L. I Have Spoken to My Children, (one act). New York: Friendship Press, 1957. NYP

TANK, Herb. Longitude 49. New York: New Playwrights, 1952. Schom

TAYLOR, Dwight, and Lawrence, Reginald. Out of This World, (musical), 1950.

WASSERMAN, Dale, & Geller, Bruce. Livin' the Life, (musical), 1957. Typescript, 1957. PAL

WILLIAMS, Tennessee. Cat on a Hot Tin Roof, 1955. New York: New American Library, 1955. PAL

WILLIAMS, Tennessee. Orpheus Descending, 1957. New York: New Directions, 1958. PAL

WILLIS, Cecil. The Velvet Plain. New York: Samuel French, 1954.

WOUK, Herman. Nature's Way, 1957. New York: Samuel French, 1958. PAL

1960 - 1970

ABEL, Lionel. The Pretender, 1960.

AFRO-AMERICAN FOLKLORIC TROUPE. High John de Conqueror, 1969.

AFRO-AMERICAN STUDIO. Where It's At, 1969.

AHMAD, Dorothy. Papa's Daughter, (one act). In The Drama Review, Vol. 12, No. 4, (Summer, 1968). PAL

ALBEE, Edward. The Death of Bessie Smith, 1961. In The Zoo Story, The Death of Bessie Smith, The Sandbox; Three Plays. New York: Coward-McCann, 1960. PAL

ALEXANDER, Robert. Nobody Loves an Albatross, 1963. New York: Dramatists Play Service, 1964. PAL

ALLAN, Steve, and Pruneau, Phillip. Sophie, (musical), 1963. In Best Plays of 1962-1963, Hewes, Henry. PAL

AMIS, Lola Jones. Helen. New York: Exposition Press, 1965. NYP

AMIS, Lola Jones. The Other Side of the Wall. New York: Exposition, 1965. NYP

AMIS, Lola Jones. The Places of Wrath. New York: Exposition Press, 1965. NYP

ANONYMOUS. A Happening with Butterfly McQueen and Her Friends, 1969.

ANONYMOUS. The Negro Speaks of Rivers, 1967.

ANTEBI, Sidney. Loop the Loop on the Moebuis Strip, (unprod.), 1965.

ARCHIBALD, William. The Cantilevered Terrace, 1962. New York: Samuel French, 1962. PAL

ARRIGHI, Mel. An Ordinary Man, 1968. New York: Dramatists Play Service, 1969.

ARTHUR, Robert Alan. Carry Me Back to Morningside Heights, 1968. In Best Plays of 1967-1968, Guernsey, Otis (ed.). PAL

ARTHUR, Robert Alan. Kwamina, 1961. In Best Plays of 1961-1962, Hewes, Henry. PAL

ARZOOMANIAN, Raffi. Still Waiting, (one act). In Ararat, No. 38, (Summer, 1969). New York: Armenian General Benevolent Union of America, 1969.

BALDWIN, James. The Amen Corner, 1965. New York: Dial Press, 1968. PAL

BALDWIN, James. Blues for Mister Charlie, 1964. New York: Dial Press, 1964. Schom

BARRETT, Nathan. The Aunts of Antioch City, (unprod.), 1964.

BARRETT, Nathan. Engagement in San Dominque, (unprod.), 1964.

BARRETT, Nathan. For Love of Mike, 1967.

BARRETT, Nathan. Lead Ball, (one act), 1965.

BARRETT, Nathan. Losers: Weepers, (one act), 1962.

BARRETT, Nathan. A Room of Roses, (unprod.), 1964.

BARRETT, Nathan. S-C-A-R-E-W-E-D, 1960. Typescript. NEC

BARRETT, Nathan. Sitting and Chipping, (one act), 1965.

BARRETT, Nathan. While Dames Dine, (one act), 1965.

BASS, George Houston. Games, (one act), 1967. In Introduction
  to Black Literature in America, Patterson, Lindsay (ed.).
  New York: The Publisher's Co., 1968. NYP

BASS, Kinsley D., Jr. We Righteous Bombers, (one act), 1968. In
  New Plays from the Black Theatre, Bullins, Ed (ed.). New York:
  Bantam Books, 1969.

BEHAN, Brendan. The Hostage, 1960. New York: Grove Press, 1964.
  PAL

BLAKE, Elizabeth. The Man Nobody Saw, (one act). In Plays for
  Living Series (a division of the Family Service Association of
  America), 1969.

BOYD, Rev. Malcolm. The Community, 1964.

BOYD, Rev. Malcolm. The Job, (one act), 1963.

BOYD, Rev. Malcolm. Study in Color, (one act), 1963.

BOYD, Rev. Malcolm. They Aren't Real to Me, (one act), 1963.

BRANCH, William. To Follow the Phoenix, 1960.

BRANCH, William. A Wreath for Udomo, 1960. Typescript. PAL

BREWSTER, Townsend J. Rudens, 1967. Typescript, 1969. NEC

BROAD, Jay. Red, White and Maddox, (musical), 1969.

BROPHY, Edmund. Nothin' to Nothin', (one act). In Best Short Plays 1960-1961, Mayorga, Margaret (ed.). Boston: Beacon Press, 1962. NYP

BROWN, Kenneth. Blake's Design, (one act), 1968. In Best Short Plays, 1969, Richards, Stanley (ed.). New York: Chilton Book Co., 1969. NYP

BROWN, Kenneth. The Brig, 1963. New York: Hill and Wang, 1965. NYP

BROWN, Oscar. Kicks and Company, (musical), 1961. In Best Plays of 1961-1962, Hewes, Henry. PAL

BRUNSON, Doris, and Furman, Roger. Three Shades of Harlem, 1964(?).

BULLINS, Ed. Clara's Ole Man, (one act), 1965. In Five Plays by Ed Bullins. Indianapolis: Bobbs-Merrill Co., 1969.

BULLINS, Ed. The Corner, (unprod.), 1967.

BULLINS, Ed. Dialect Determinism, (one act), 1965. Typescript. NEC

BULLINS, Ed. The Duplex, 1969.

BULLINS, Ed. The Electronic Nigger, (one act), 1966. In Five Plays by Ed Bullins. Indianapolis: Bobbs-Merrill Co., 1969.

BULLINS, Ed, and Tarbell, Shirley. The Game of Adam and Eve, (one act), 1966. Typescript. NEC

BULLINS, Ed. The Gentleman Caller, (one act), 1966.

BULLINS, Ed. Goin' a Buffalo, 1966. In Five Plays by Ed Bullins. Indianapolis: Bobbs-Merrill Co., 1969.

BULLINS, Ed. The Helper, (one act), 1966. Typescript. NEC

BULLINS, Ed. How Do You Do: A Nonsense Drama, (one act), 1965. Mill Valley, California: Illuminations Press, 1967.

BULLINS, Ed. In the Wine Time, 1966. In Five Plays by Ed Bullins. Indianapolis: Bobbs-Merrill Co., 1969.

BULLINS, Ed. It Has No Choice, (one act), 1966.

BULLINS, Ed. The Man Who Dug Fish, 1967.

BULLINS, Ed. A Minor Scene, (one act), 1966. Typescript. NEC

BULLINS, Ed. In New England Winter, 1967. In New Plays from
the Black Theatre, Bullins, Ed (ed.). New York: Bantam Books,
1969.

BULLINS, Ed. The Pig Pen, 1970. APT

BULLINS, Ed. A Son Come Home, (one act), 1968. In Five Plays
by Ed Bullins. Indianapolis: Bobbs-Merrill Co., 1969.

BULLINS, Ed. The Theme is Blackness, (one act), (unprod.). Typescript,
1966. NEC

CALDWELL, Ben. The Fanatic, (one act), 1968.

CALDWELL, Ben. The First Militant Preacher, (one act), 1969. Newark,
N.J.: Jihad Press, 1967.

CALDWELL, Ben. Hypnotism, (one act), 1966. In Afro Arts
Anthology. Newark, N.J.: Jihad Press, 1966.

CALDWELL, Ben. The Job, (one act), 1966. In The Drama Review, Vol.
12, No. 4, (Summer, 1968). PAL

CALDWELL, Ben. The King of Soul, or The Devil and Otis Redding, (one
act), 1968. In Black Theatre, No. 3, Bullins, Ed (ed.). New York:
New Lafayette Theatre Publications, 1969.

CALDWELL, Ben. Mission Accomplished, (one act), 1967. In The
Drama Review, Vol. 12, No. 4, (Summer, 1968). PAL

CALDWELL, Ben. Recognition, (one act), 1968.

CALDWELL, Ben. Riot Sale or Dollar Psyche, (one act), 1966. In
The Drama Review, Vol. 12, No. 4, (Summer, 1968). PAL

CALDWELL, Ben. Top Secret, (one act). In The Drama Review, Vol.
12, No. 4, (Summer, 1968). PAL

CALDWELL, Ben. Unpresidented, (one act), 1968.

CALDWELL, Ben. The Wall, (one act), 1967.

CANNON, Alice. Great Day in the Morning, 1962. New York: Samuel French, 1964. PAL

CARLINO, Lewis J. The Dirty Old Man, (one act), 1964. New York: Random House, 1964. PAL

CARLINO, Lewis. Sarah and the Sax, (one act), 1964. New York: Random House, 1964. PAL

CARROLL, Vinnette. But Never Jam Today, 1969.

CARROLL, Vinnette. Trumpets of the Lord, 1963. In Best Plays of 1963-1964, Hewes, Henry. PAL

CARTER, Steve. As You Can See, (one act), 1968.

CARTER, Steve. The Terraced Apartment, (one act), 1968.

CHARMIN, Martin, and Rodgers, Mary. Hot Spot, (musical), 1963. In Best Plays of 1962-1963, Hewes, Henry. PAL

CHILDRESS, Alice. Strings, (one act), 1969. NEC

CHILDRESS, Alice. Young Martin Luther King, Jr., 1969.

CHISOLM, Earle. Black Manhood, 1970.

COOK, Richard. The Seduction or Innocence Preserved. Typescript, 1966. NEC

CROWLEY, Mart. The Boys in the Band, 1968. New York: Dell, 1969.

CULLINAN, Thomas. Mrs. Lincoln, 1968. New York: Dramatists Play Service, 1969.

CURTIS, Pat and Norman. Walk Down Mah Street, (musical), 1968.

DALLAS THEATRE CENTER RESIDENT COMPANY. White on White, (one act), 1969. Typescript. PAL

DANIEL, Gloria. The Male Bag, 1970.

DA SILVA, Howard, and Leon, Felix. The Zulu and the Zayda, 1965.
New York: Dramatists Play Service, 1966. PAL

DAVIDSON, Barbara. The Children Are Listening, (one act), 1962.

DAVIDSON, N.R. Jr. El Hajj Malik, (one act), 1968. In New
Plays from the Black Theatre, Bullins, Ed (ed.). New York:
Bantam Books, 1969.

DAVIDSON, William F. Learn, Baby, Learn. Chicago: Dramatic
Publishing Co., 1969.

DAVIS, Milburn. The $100,000 Nigger, (unprod.), 1969.

DAVIS, Milburn. Sometimes a Switchblade, (one act), 1969.

DAVIS, Ossie. Curtain Call Mr. Aldrich Sir, (one act), 1963.
In The Black Teacher and the Dramatic Arts, Reardon and Pawley,
(eds.). New York: Negro University Press, 1970.

DAVIS, Ossie. Purlie Victorious, 1961. New York: Samuel French,
1961. PAL

DAVIS, Ossie. What Can You Say to Mississippi?, (one act), 1955.

DAVIS, Ron G., and Landau, Saul. A Minstrel Show; or, Civil
Rights in a Cracker Barrel, 1965.

DEAN, Philip Hayes. Every Night When the Sun Goes Down, 1969. APT

DEAN, Philip Hayes. This Bird of Dawning Singeth All Night Long,
(one act), 1968. APT

DELANEY, Shelagh. A Taste of Honey, 1960. New York: Grove Press,
1962. PAL

DENKER, Henry. What Did We Do Wrong?, 1967. New York:
Samuel French, 1967.

DENT, Tom. Negro Study #34A, (one act), 1969. FST

DENT, Tom. Riot Duty, (one act), 1969. FST

DENT, Tom. Ritual Murder, (one act), 1967. FST

DENT, Tom. Snapshot, (one act), 1969. FST

DENT, Tom, and Ferdinand, Val. Song of Survival, (one act), 1969.
FST

DENTZIN. Paris...Fall. Typescript, 1967. NEC

DINARDO, Robert E. Empress of the Blues. Typescript, 1965. NEC

DINROE, Dorothy, and Walker, Joseph. Ododo, 1968. Typescript.
NEC

DODSON, Owen. 'Till Victory is Won, (opera), 1967.

DOLAN, Harry. Losers Weepers, (one act). In From the Ashes:
Voices of Watts, Schulberg, Budd (ed.). New York:
Meridian Books, 1969.

DOUGLAS, Rodney. Voice of the Ghetto. New York: Samuel French,
1968.

DUBERMAN, Martin. In White America, 1963. Boston: Houghton, 1964.

EISENSTEIN, Mark. The Fighter, 1958. In Four New Yale Playwrights,
Gassner, John (ed.). New York: Crown Publishers, 1965. PAL

ELDER, Lonne, III. Ceremonies in Dark Old Men, 1965. New York:
Noonday Press, 1969. PAL

ELDER, Lonne, III. Charades on East Fourth Street, (one act), 1967.

ELDER, Lonne, III. A Hysterical Turtle in A Rabbit Race, (unprod.),
1961.

ELDER, Lonne, III. Kissin' Rattlesnakes Can Be Fun, (one act), 1966.

ELDER, Lonne, III. Seven Comes Up, Seven Comes Down, (one act),
1966.

FALLON, T. A Dead Geranium. Typescript, 1968. NEC

FAST, Howard. The Hill. New York: Doubleday, 1964. PAL

FERDINAND, Val. Black Liberation Army, (one act), 1969. FST

FERDINAND, Val. Cop Killer, (one act), 1968. FST

FERDINAND, Val. Happy Birthday, Jesus, (one act), 1968. FST

FERDINAND, Val. Homecoming, (one act), 1969. FST

FERDINAND, Val. Picket, (one act), 1968. FST

FERDINAND, Val. Mama, (one act), 1968. FST

FERDINAND, Val, and Dent, Tom. Song of Survival, (one act), 1969. FST

FIEBLEMAN, Peter. Tiger, Tiger, Burning Bright, 1961. Cleveland: World Publishing Co., 1963. Schom

FLAGG, Ann. Great Gettin' Up Mornin', (one act). New York: Samuel French, 1964. NYP

FORSYTH, James. Defiant Island, 1962.

FOSTER, Alex. Community Kitchen, 1968.

FOWLER, John T. The Sound of Drums. Typescript, 1967. NEC

FRIEDMAN, Bruce Jay. Scuba Duba, 1967. New York: Simon and Schuster, 1968. Schom/DPS

FRINGS, Ketti. The Long Dream, 1960. In Best Plays of 1959-1960, Kronenberger, Louis. PAL

FUGARD, Athol. The Blood Knot, 1963. New York: Odyssey Press, 1964.

FUGARD, Athole. The Occupation, (one act). In Ten One Act Plays, Pieters, Cosmo (ed.). African Writers Series #34. London: Heinemann Educational Books, Ltd., 1968.

FULLER, Charles. Ain't Nobody Sarah But Me (The Sunflowers), (one act), 1969.

FULLER, Charles. Cabin (The Sunflowers), (one act), 1969.

FULLER, Charles. The Conductor, (unprod.), 1969.

FULLER, Charles. Indian Giver (The Sunflowers), (one act), 1969.

FULLER, Charles. JJ's Game (The Sunflowers), (one act), 1969.

FULLER, Charles. The Layout (The Sunflowers), (one act), 1968.

FULLER, Charles. Love Song For Robert Lee, (one act), 1968.

FULLER, Charles. Perfect Party (The Village: A Party), 1969.

FULLER, Charles. The Rise, (unprod.), 1967.

FULLER, Charles. The Sunflower Majorette (The Sunflowers), 1969.

FURMAN, Roger, and Brunson, Doris. Three Shades of Harlem, 1964(?).

GARRETT, Jimmy. And We Own the Night, (one act), 1967. In The Drama Review, Vol. 12, No. 4, (Summer, 1968). PAL

GARSON, Barbara. MacBird, 1967. New York: Grove Press, 1967.

GARVIN, Larry, and Morales, Aida, and Hatch, James. The Conspiracy, 1970. PAL

GELBER, Jack. The Apple, 1961. New York: Grove Press, 1961. NYP

GENET, Jean. The Blacks, 1961. Grove Press, 1960. PAL

GEOGHEGAN, J.J. Decision at Tongo, 1963.

GIBSON, William & Odets, Clifford. Golden Boy, (musical), 1964. New York: Atheneum, 1965. PAL

GILLEN, Leon. The Rose Man. Typescript, 1966. NEC

GLENN, Robert, and Johnson, James W. God's Trombones, 1960.

GORDONE, Charles. No Place to be Somebody, 1969. Indianapolis: Bobbs-Merrill, 1969.

GORDONE, Charles. Worl's Champeen Lip Dansuh an' Wahtah Mellon Jooglah, (unprod.), 1969.

GREEN LANTERN HOUSE PLAYERS. Cool Niggers, 1969.

GREEN, Paul. The Stephen Foster Story. New York: Samuel French, 1960. NYP

GREENBERG, Dan, and Vall, Seymour. How To Be A Jewish Mother, 1967. In Best Plays of 1967-1968, Guernsey, Otis L. Jr. PAL

GREENE, Otis. A Different Part of the World, (unprod.), 1967.

GREENFELD, Josh. Clandestine on the Morning Line, 1961. New York: Dramatists Play Service, 1961. PAL

GREENWOOD, Frank. Burn, Baby, Burn!, 1966.

GUNN, Bill. Johnnas, (one act). In The Drama Review, Vol. 12, No. 4 (Summer, 1968). PAL

GUNN, Bill. Marcus in the High Grass, 1960. PAL

HAIRSTON, William. The Honeymooners, (one act). Typescript, 1967. NEC

HAIRSTON, William. Walk in Darkness, 1963. Typescript, 1963. PAL

HALSEY, William. Judgement, (one act). In Black Dialogue Magazine, Vol. IV, No. 1, (Spring, 1969). New York: Black Dialogue Publications, 1969.

HANLEY, William. Slow Dance on the Killing Ground, 1964. New York: Random House, 1965. NYP/DPS

HANSBERRY, Lorraine. The Sign in Sidney Brustein's Window, 1964. New York: Random House, 1965. NYP/SF

HANSBERRY, Lorraine. To Be Young, Gifted, and Black, 1969. Englewood Cliffs, N.J.: Prentice-Hall, Inc., 1969.

HARRIS, Tom. All the Tigers are Tame, (unprod.), 1960.

HARRIS, Tom. Always with Love (Mothers Little Helper), 1967. In New American Plays, Vol. 4. New York: Hill and Wang, 1969.

HARRIS, Tom. Beverly Hills Olympics, (unprod.), 1964.

HARRIS, Tom. City Beneath the Skin, (unprod.), 1961.

HARRIS, Tom. Cleaning Day, (one act), 1969.

HARRIS, Tom. Daddy Hugs and Kisses, (one act), 1963.

HARRIS, Tom. Death of Daddy Hugs and Kisses, (unprod.), 1963.

HARRIS, Tom. Divorce Negro Style, (unprod.), 1968.

HARRIS, Tom. The Golden Spear, (one act), 1969.

HARRIS, Tom. Moving Day, (one act), 1969.

HARRIS, Tom. The Relic, 1967.

HARRIS, Tom. Shopping Day, (one act), 1969.

HARRIS, Tom. Who Killed Sweetie, (unprod.), 1967.

HARRISON, Paul Carter. Tabernacle. In New Black Playwrights,
   Couch, William, Jr. (ed.). New York: Avon Books, 1970.

HATCH, James V. and Jackson, C.B. Fly Blackbird, (musical), 1960.
   In The Black Teacher and the Dramatic Arts, Reardon and Pawley
   (eds.). New York: Negro University Press, 1970.

HATCH, James, and Garvin, Larry, and Morales, Aida.
   The Conspiracy, 1970. PAL

HELLMAN, Lillian. My Mother, My Father and Me, 1963. New York:
   Random House, 1963. PAL/DPS

HELLMAN, Lillian. Toys in the Attic, 1960. New York: Random House,
   1960. PAL/SF

HILL, Abram. Split Down the Middle, (unprod.). New York: Simon
   and Schuster, 1970.

HILL, Mars. The Huzzy, (one act). Typescript, 1969. NEC

HOGAN, Frank. The Assassination of Martin Luther King, (one act),
   1968.

HUGHES, Langston. Black Nativity, 1961.

HUGHES, Langston. The Gospel Glory: A Passion Play. Typescript,
   1962. Schom

HUGHES, Langston. Jerico-Jim-Crow, (a song play), 1964. Typescript,
   1963. PAL

HUGHES, Langston. The Prodigal Son, (one act), 1965. In Players Magazine,
   Vol. 43, No. 2, (December 1967-January, 1968). PAL

HUGHES, Langston. Tambourines to Glory, 1963. In Five Plays by
Langston Hughes, Smalley, Webster (ed.). Bloomington:
Indiana University Press, 1968. PAL

HUGHES, Langston, and Teaque, Bob. Soul Yesterday and Today, 1969.

HULT, Ruby. The Saga of George W. Bush. In Negro Digest,
(September, 1962). Schom

IMAN, Yusef. Praise the Lord, But Pass the Ammunition, (one act).
Newark, N.J.: Jihad Pulbication, 196?

ISHERWOOD, Christopher. The Adventures of the Black Girl in Search
for God, 1969.

JACKSON, C.B. and Hatch, James V. Fly Blackbird, (musical),
1960. In The Black Teacher and the Dramatic Arts, Reardon and
Pawley, (eds.). New York: Negro University Press, 1970.

JACKSON, Josephine and Walker, Joseph. The Believers, 1968.
In Best Plays of 1967-1968, Guernsey, Otis L. Jr. PAL

JANKE, Hal. Free At Last. Typescript, 1968. NEC

JASUADOWICZ, Dennis. Blood Money, (one act). In New American
Plays, Vol 1, Corrigan, Robert (ed.). New York: Hill and Wang,
1965.

JASUDOWICZ, Dennis. Slumming, (one act). In Tulane Drama Review,
Vol. 9, No. 2, (Winter, 1964). PAL

JOHN, Errol. Moon on a Rainbow Shawl, 1962. London: Faber, 1958.

JOHNSON, James W. and Glenn, Robert. God's Trombones, 1960.

JONES, LeRoi. Arm Yrself or Harm Yrself, (one act), 196? Newark,
N.J.: Jihad Press, 196? Schom

JONES, LeRoi. The Baptism, (one act), 1964. New York: Grove Press, 1964. PAL

JONES, LeRoi. A Black Mass, (one act), 1966. In Four Black Revolutionary Plays. Indianapolis: Bobbs-Merrill, 1969.

JONES, LeRoi. Board of Education, (one act), 1968.

JONES, LeRoi. B.P. Chant, (one act), 1968.

JONES, LeRoi. Chant, (one act), 1968.

JONES, LeRoi. Dante, (one act), 1964. In Systems of Dante's Hell. New York: Grove Press, 1965. NYP

JONES, LeRoi. Dutchman, (one act), 1964. New York: Wm. Morrow & Co., 1964. PAL

JONES, LeRoi. Experimental Death Unit #1, (one act), 1965. In Four Black Revolutionary Plays. Indianapolis: Bobbs-Merrill, 1969.

JONES, LeRoi. Great Goodness of Life, (A Coon Show), 1967. In Best Short Plays of the World Theatre, 1958-1967, Richards, Stanley (ed.). New York: Crown Publishers, Inc., 1968. PAL

JONES, LeRoi. Home on the Range, (one act), 1967. In The Drama Review, Vol. 12, No. 4, (Summer, 1968). PAL

JONES, LeRoi. Insurrection, (one act), 1968.

JONES, LeRoi. J-E-L-L-O, (one act), 1965. Newark, N.J.: Jihad Press, 1970(?).

JONES, LeRoi. Junkies are Full of Shhhh, (one act), 1969.

JONES, LeRoi. The Kid Poeta Tragical, (unprod.), 1969.

JONES, LeRoi. Madheart, (one act), 1966. In Four Black Revolutionary Plays, Indianapolis: Bobbs-Merrill, 1969.

JONES, LeRoi. Police, (one act). In The Drama Review, Vol. 12, No. 4, (Summer, 1968). PAL

JONES, LeRoi. A Recent Killing, (unprod.?), 1964.

JONES, LeRoi. The Slave, (one act), 1964. New York: Wm.
Morrow & Co., 1964. NYP

JONES, LeRoi. The Slave Ship, 1969. Newark, N.J.: Jihad
Productions, 1969.

JONES, LeRoi. The Toilet, (one act), 1964. New York: Grove
Press, 1963. PAL

JOSEPH, Robert. Face of a Hero, 1960. The Theatre, Vol. 2, No.
10, (October, 1960). PAL

KAMINSKY, Marc. Little Korea, A Fair Hearing. Typescript,
1969. NEC

KENNEDY, Adrienne. A Beast's Story, 1966.

KENNEDY, Adrienne. Cities of Bezique, 1969.

KENNEDY, Adrienne. The Funnyhouse of a Negro, (one act), 1964.
In Anthology of the American Negro in the Theatre, Patterson,
Lindsay (ed.). New York: The Publisher's Co., 1967. PAL

KENNEDY, Adrienne. A Lesson in a Dead Language, 1964.

KENNEDY, Adrienne. The Owl Answers, 1963.

KENNEDY, Adrienne. A Rat's Mass, (one act), 1966. In New
Black Playwrights, Couch, William (ed.). Baton Rouge:
Louisiana State University, 1968. PAL

KILLENS, John O. Lower Than the Angels, 1965. APT

KILLENS, John O., and Mitchell, Loften. Ballad of the
Winter Soldiers, 1965.

KING, Charles H. Voices of Liberty, 1966.

KINGSLEY, Sidney. Night Life, 1962. New York: Dramatists
Play Service, 1966. PAL

KIRKLAND, Jack. Mandingo, 1961. In Best Plays of 1960-1961,
Kronenberger, Louis. PAL

KOENIG, Laird. The Dozens, 1969.

LANDAU, Saul, and Davis, Ron G. A Minstrel Show; or, Civil Rights in a Cracker Barrel, 1965.

LAURENTS, Arthur. Hallelujah Baby, 1967. Typescript. PAL

LEMAY, Harding. Look At Any Man, 1963. In Best Plays of 1963-1964, Hewes, Henry. PAL

LEON, Felix, and Da Silva, Howard. The Zulu and the Zayda, 1965. New York: Dramatists Play Service, 1966. PAL

LEVIN, Ira. Critic's Choice, 1960. New York: Random House, 1961. PAL/DPS

LEWIS, David. Georgia Man and Jamaican Woman, 1969.

LITT, David. Thyestes. Typescript, 1968. NEC

LOWELL, Robert. Benito Cereno, 1964. In Theatre Experiment, Benedict, M. (ed.). Garden City, New York: Doubleday, 1967.

MACBETH, Robert. A Black Ritual. In Black Theatre, No. 2, Bullins, Ed (ed.). New York: New Lafayette Theatre Publication, 1969.

MCCORMACK, Tom. American Roulette, 1969. New York: Dramatists Play Service, 1969.

MCCRAY, Nettle (also known as Salimu). Growin' Into Blackness, (one act), 1969. In Black Theatre, No. 2, Bullins, Ed (ed.). New York: New Lafayette Theatre Publications, 1969.

MCIVER, Ray. God Is A (Guess What?), 1968. NEC

MACK, Ron. Black is ...We Are, 1969.

MACKEY, William. Behold! Cometh the Vanderkellans, 1965. Typescript. PAL

MACKEY, William. Family Meeting. In New Black Playwrights, Couch, William (ed.). Baton Rouge: Louisiana State University, 1968. PAL

MALCOLM, Barbara (also known as Nayo). Fourth Generation, (one act), 1969. FST

MANHOFF, Bill. The Owl and the Pussycat, 1965. New York: Samuel French, 1965.

MARK, Norman. The Integrators, (one act). New York:
Samuel French, 1966.

MARTIE, Charles. Where We At, 1969.

MASON, Clifford. Jimmy X.

MATISSE, O. Vernon. The Blues for Molly Baker, (unprod.), 1961.
Typescript.

MARVIN X. The Resurrection of the Dead, (in four movements).
In Black Theatre, No. 3, Bullins, Ed (ed.). New York:
New Lafayette Theatre Publications, 1969.

MARVIN X. Take Care of Business, (one act), 196? In The Drama
Review, Vol. 12, No. 4, (Summer, 1968). PAL

MELFI, Leonard. The Shirt, (one act). In Encounters. New York:
Random House, 1967. PAL

MILLER, Arthur. After the Fall, 1964. New York: Viking Press, 1964.
PAL/DPS

MILLER, Laura Ann. The Cricket Cries, (one act), 1967.

MILLER, Laura Ann. The Echo of a Sound, (one act), 1968.

MILLER, Laura Ann. Fannin Road, Straight Ahead, (unprod.), 1968.

MILLER, Laura Ann. Git Away From Here Irvine, Now Git,
(unprod.), 1969.

MILLER, Warren and Rossen, Robert. The Cool World, 1960. In
Best Plays of 1959-1960, Kronenberger, Louis. PAL

MILNER, Ronald. The Monster, (one act). In The Drama Review, Vol.
12, No. 4, (Summer, 1968). PAL

MILNER, Ron. The Warning - A Theme for Linda, 1969.

MILNER, Ronald. Who's Got His Own, 1966. Typescript. PAL

MITCHELL, Loften. And the Walls Came Tumbling Down, (unprod.),
1969(?).
MITCHELL, Loften. Ballad of a Blackbird, (musical), (unprod.),
1968.

MITCHELL, Loften. The Phonograph, 1961.

MITCHELL, Loften. Star of the Morning, 1964(?).

MITCHELL, Loften. Tell Pharoah, 1967. New York: Negro
   University Press, 1970.

MITCHELL, Loften. The World of a Harlem Playwright, 1968.

MITCHELL, Loften and Killens, John O. Ballad of the Winter
   Soldiers, 1965.

MITCHELL, Louis D. Horse's Play.

MITCHELL, Melvin L. The American Cartoon.

MOLETTE, Carlton II. Doctor B.S. Black, 1969.

MORALES, Aida, and Hatch, James, and Garvin, Larry.
   The Conspiracy, 1970. PAL

MOSES, Gilbert. Roots, (one act). In The Free Southern Theatre,
   Dent, Thomas; Moses, Gilbert; Schechner, Richard (eds.).
   Indianapolis: Bobbs-Merrill, 1969.

MOSIER, Frank M. The Duchess of Santiago, (unprod.), 1967.

MULHOLLAND, Catherine. The Lincoln Memorial. Typescript, 1967.
   NEC

NEAL, Larry. The Suppression of Jazz.

NEW HERITAGE REPERTORY THEATRE. Hip, Black, and Angry, 1968.

NICHOL, James W. Sweet Home Sweet, (one act). Typescript, 1967.
   NEC

O'BRIEN, Conor Cruise. Murderous Angles, 1970. Boston:
   Little Brown, 1968.

ODETS, Clifford, & Gibson, William. Golden Boy, (musical),
   1964. New York: Atheneum, 1965. PAL

PANAS, Alexander. Mr. Tambo, Mr. Bones, 1969.

PATON, Alan and Shah, Krishna. Sponono, 1964. Typescript.
   PAL

PAWLEY, Thomas D. _FFV_, 1963.

PAWLEY, Thomas D. _The Tumult and the Shouting_, 1969.

PLOMER, William. _I Speak of Africa: Two Plays for a Puppet Theatre_ ("The Triumph of Justice", and "The Man in the Corner"). In _Drama Critique_, (The Negro in the Theatre), (Spring, 1964). Schom

PORTMAN, Julie and Rollins, Bryant. _Riot_, 1968.

PRUNEAU, Phillip and Allan, Steve. _Sophie_, (musical), 1963. In _Best Plays of 1962-1963_, Hewes, Henry. PAL

RADO, James, and Ragni, Gerome. _Hair_, 1965. New York: Pocket Books, Inc., 1969.

RAGNI, Gerome, and Rado, James. _Hair_, 1965. New York: Pocket Books, Inc., 1969.

RAMA RAU, Santha. _A Passage to India_, 1962. New York: Harcourt, 1960. PAL

RAPHAEL, Lennox. _Che_, 1968. North Hollywood, California: Contact Books, 1969.

RAPHLING, Sam. _President Lincoln_, (opera), (unprod.), 1962.

RAYFIEL, David. _P.S. 193_, 1962. In _Best Plays of 1962-1963_, Hewes, Henry. PAL

REARDON, William R. _Never Etch in Acid_, 1969.

REED, Edwena. _A Man Always Keeps His Word_, (one act). _Negro History Bulletin_, Vol. XXVI, No. 4, (January, 1963). NYP

REID, William D. _The Plague_.

REINER, Carl. _Something Different_, 1967. In _Best Plays of 1967-1968_, Guernsey, Otis L. Jr. PAL/SF

ROACH, Freddie. _Soul Pieces_, 1969.

ROBERSON, Arthur. _Don't Leave Go My Hand_, 1969.

ROBERSON, Arthur. In the Shadow of Ham, (unprod.), 1968.

ROBERSON, Arthur. Melanosis, (unprod.),(one act), 1969.

ROBERSON, Arthur. Run Sweet Child to Silence, (unprod.),
1968.

RODALE, J.I. The Goose, 1960. Typescript, 1960. PAL

RODGERS, Mary, and Charmin, Martin. Hot Spot, (musical),
1963. In Best Plays of 1962-1963, Hewes, Henry. PAL

RODGERS, Richard, and Taylor, Samuel. No Strings, 1962.
New York: Random House, 1962. PAL

ROGERS, David. If That's Where It's At, Baby, I'm Not Going.
Chicago: The Dramatic Publishing Co., 1969.

ROLLINS, Bryant and Portman, Julie. Riot, 1968.

ROSE, Reginald. Black Monday. Typescript. PAL

ROSS, John M. Aztec Qzin, 1968.

ROSS, John M. House or No House, 1967.

ROSS, John M. I Will Repay, 1963.

ROSSEN, Robert and Miller, Warren. The Cool World, 1960.
In Best Plays of 1959-1960, Kronenberger, Louis. PAL

ROTHBERGER, Morton. Black History from the Jewish Point of
View, 1969.

RUSSELL, Charlie L. Five on the Black Hand Side, 1969. APT

SACKLER, Howard. The Great White Hope, 1968. New York:
Bantam Books, 1968.

ST. CLAIR, Wesley. The Station, (one act), 1969.

SANCHEZ, Sonia. The Bronx is Next, (one act). In The
Drama Review, Vol. 12, No. 4. (Summer, 1968). PAL

SANCHEZ, Sonia. Sister Son/ji, (one act), 1969. In
New Plays from the Black Theatre, Bullins, Ed (ed.).
New York: Bantam Books, 1969.

SANDERS, James. Next Time I'll Sing to You, 1963. New York: Random House, 1963. PAL

SAPIN, Louis. Daddy Goodness, 1968. Typescript. PAL

SAROYAN, William. Death Along the Wabash, (one act), 1961. In Three Along the Wabash. Typescript, 1961. PAL

SAROYAN, William. Hanging Around the Wabash, (one act), 1961. In Three Along the Wabash. Typescript, 1961. PAL

SAROYAN, William. High Time Along the Wabash, (one act), 1961. In Three Along the Wabash. Typescript, 1961. PAL

SAUTER, Joe and Sawyer, Mike, and Brandon, Johnny. Cindy, (musical), 1964. In Best Plays of 1963-1964, Hewes, Henry. PAL

SAWYER, Mike and Sauter, Joe, and Brandon, Johnny. Cindy, (musical), 1964. In Best Plays of 1963-1964, Hewes, Henry. PAL

SCHEVILL, James. The Black President. Denver: Alan Swallow, 1965. PAL

SCHOCHEN, Seyril. The Moon Besieged, 1962. In Best Plays of 1962-1963, Hewes, Henry. PAL

SCHULBERG, Budd and Stuart. What Makes Sammy Run?, 1964. New York: Random House, 1965. PAL

SELF, Charles. The Smokers, (one act), 1966. FST

SERGEL, Christopher. Up the Down Staircase. Chicago: The Dramatic Publishing Co., 1969.

SEWELL, E.G. The Voice from Dunberry Hill. Typescript, 1964. NEC

SHAH, Krishna, and Paton, Alan. Sponono, 1964. Typescript. PAL

SHEPP, Archie. June Bug Graduates Tonight, 1967.

SHEPP, Archie. Revolution, 1968.

SHINE, Ted. The Coca-Cola Boys, (one act), (unprod.), 1969.

SHINE, Ted. Comeback After the Fire, 1969.

SHINE, Ted. Contribution, (one act), 1969.

SHINE, Ted. Flora's Kisses, (one act), 1969.

SHINE, Ted. Hamburgers At Hamburger Heaven Are
    Impersonal, (one act), (unprod.), 1969.

SHINE, Ted. Idabel's Fortune, (one act), 1969.

SHINE, Ted. Jeanne West, (musical), (unprod.), 1968.

SHINE, Ted. Miss Victoria, (one act), (unprod.), 1965.

SHINE, Ted. Morning, Noon, and Night, 1964. In The Black
    Teacher and the Dramatic Arts, Reardon, William and Pawley,
    Thomas (eds.). New York: Negro University Press, 1970.

SHINE, Ted. Plantation, (one act), 1970.

SHINE, Ted. Pontiac, (one act), (unprod.), 1967.

SHINE, Ted. Shoes, (one act), 1969. In Encore Magazine,
    Vol. XII (Tallahassee: Florida A&M University, 1969).

SHINE, Ted. Waiting Room, (one act), (unprod.), 1969.

SHURTLEFF, Michael. Call Me By My Rightful Name. Typescript,
    1960. PAL/DPS

SKLAR, George. And People All Around, 1966. New York:
    Random House, 1967. PAL

SOFOWOTE, Segun. Sailor Boy in Town, (one act). Oshogbo,
    Nigeria: Theatre Express Sketches, 1966. Schom

SOYINKA, Wole. Dance of the Forests. In Five Plays. London:
    Three Crown Books (Oxford University Press), 1965.

SOYINKA, Wole. Kongi's Harvest. London: Three Crown
    Books (Oxford University Press), 1967.

SOYINKA, Wole. The Lion and the Jewel. In Five Plays.
    London: Three Crown Books (Oxford University Press), 1965.

SOYINKA, Wole. The Road. London: Three Crown Books
    (Oxford University Press), 1965.

SOYINKA, Wole. The Strong Breed, (one act), 1967. New York:
    Dramatists Play Service, 1969.

SOYINKA, Wole. The Swamp Dwellers. In Five Plays. London: Three Crowns Books (Oxford University Press), 1965.

SOYINKA, Wole. The Trials of Brother Jero, (one act), 1967. New York: Dramatists Play Service, 1969.

SPENSLEY, Philip. The Nitty Gritty of Mr. Charlie, 1969.

STANBACK, Thurman. A Change Has Got to Come, (unprod.), 1969.

STEWART, Ron. Sambo (A Nigger Opera), 1969.

STOCKARD, Sharon. Proper and Fine, (one act), 1968. FST

STOKES, Herbert (also known as Damu). The Man Who Trusted The Devil Twice, (one act), 1969. In New Plays from the Black Theatre, Bullins, Ed (ed.). New York: Bantam Books, 1969.

STOKES, Herbert (also known as Damu). The Uncle Toms, (one act). In The Drama Review, Vol. 12, No. 4, (Summer, 1968). PAL

STRONG, Romaner Jack. A Date with the Intermediary, 1968.

STRONG, Romaner Jack. A Direct Confrontation in Black, (one act), 1968.

STRONG, Romaner Jack. Mesmerism of a Maniac, 1967.

STRONG, Romaner Jack. The Psychedelic Play or a Happening, (one act), 1967.

STRONG, Romaner Jack. Metamorphisms, (one act), 1966.

TABORI, George. The Niggerlovers, (two short plays: "The Demonstration," and "Man and Dog"), 1967. In The Best Plays of 1967-1968, Guernsey, Otis L. PAL

TARBELL, Shirley, and Bullins, Ed. The Game of Adam and Eve, (one act). Typescript. NEC

TAYLOR, Samuel, and Rogers, Richard. No Strings, 1962. New York: Random House, 1962. PAL

TEAQUE, Bob, and Hughes, Langston. Soul Yesterday and Today, 1969.

THEATRE BLACK. For My People, 1968.

THOM, Robert. Bicycle Ride to Nevada, 1963. In Best Plays of 1963-1964, Hewes, Henry. PAL

THOMPSON, Jay. The Bible Salesman, (one act), 1961. In Theatre Arts Magazine, (July, 1961). PAL

THOMPSON, Jay. The Oldest Trick in the World, 1961. In Theatre Arts Magazine, (July, 1961). PAL

TOUSSAINT, Richard. These Black Ghettos, 1969.

TRENIER, Diane. Rich Black Heritage, (one act), (unprod.), 1970.

TUOTTI, Joseph D. Big Time Buck White, 1968. New York: Grove Press, 1969.

TUOTTI, Joseph. Buck White, (musical), 1969.

ULLMAN, Marvin. ...and I am Black, 1969.

VALL, Seymour, and Greenberg, Dan. How To Be A Jewish Mother, 1967. In Best Plays of 1967-1968, Guernsey, Otis L. Jr. PAL

VAN DOREN, Mark. The Last Days of Lincoln. In Three Distinctive Plays About Abe Lincoln, Swire, Willard (ed.). New York: Washington Square Press, 1961.

VAN SCOTT, Gloria. Poetic Suite on Arabs and Israelis, 1969. Typescript. PAL

WALKER, Evan. Coda for the Blues, (unprod.), 1968.

WALKER, Evan. Dark Light in May, (unprod.), (one act), 1960.

WALKER, Evan. East of Jordan, 1969.

WALKER, Evan. The Message, (one act), 1969.

WALKER, Evan. A War for Brutus, (unprod.), 1958.

WALKER, Joseph, and Jackson, Josephine. The Believers, 1968. In Best Plays of 1967-1968, Guernsey, Otis L. Jr. PAL

WALKER, Joseph. The Harangues, (three one acts,), 1969. APT

WALKER, Joseph, and Dinroe, Dorothy. Ododo, 1968.
Typescript. NEC

WARD, Douglas Turner. Day of Absence, (one act), 1966.
In New Black Playwrights, Couch, William (ed.).
Baton Rouge: Louisiana State University, 1968. PAL/DPS

WARD, Douglas Turner. Happy Ending, (one act), 1966. In
New Black Playwrights, Couch, William (ed.). Baton
Rouge: Louisiana State University, 1968. PAL/DPS

WARD, Douglas T. The Reckoning, 1969. NEC

WASHBURN, Deric. The Love Nest, 1963. In Best Plays of
1962-1963, Hewes, Henry. PAL

WASHINGTON, Sam. Almitra, (unprod.), 1968.

WASHINGTON, Sam. A Member of the Fateful Gray, 1969.

WASSERMAN, Dale. One Flew Over the Cuckoo's Nest, 1963.
In Best Plays of 1963-1964, Hewes, Henry. PAL/SF

WATERS, Richard D. New Shoes for Uncle Tom, 1968.

WEBER, Adam. Spirit of the Living Dead, (one act), 1969. FST

WEBER, Adam. To Kill or Die, (one act), 1969. FST

WEISS, Peter. Song of the Lusitanian Bogey. In Two Plays
by Peter Weiss. New York: Atheneum, 1970.

WELLES, Orson. Moby Dick, 1962. New York: Samuel
French, 1965. PAL

WESLEY, Richard. Springtime High, (one act), 1968(?).

WESTHEIMER, David. My Sweet Charlie, 1966. New York:
Samuel French, 1967. PAL

WHITE, Edgar. The Cathedral at Chartres, (one act), 1969.

WHITE, Edgar. The Mummer's Play, (one act), 1969.

WHITE, Edmund. The Blue Boy in Black, 1963. In Best Plays
of 1962-1963, Hewes, Henry. PAL

WHITE, Joseph. The Leader, (one act), 1969.

WHITE, Joseph. Ole Judge Moses is Dead, (one act), 1969.
In The Drama Review, Vol. 12, No. 4, (Summer, 1968). PAL

WHITE, Liz. Cooling Waters, 1962.

WHITFIELD, Vantile (also known as Motojicho). The Creeps, (one
act), 1960.

WHITFIELD, Vantile (also known as Motojicho). In Sickness
and in Health, (unprod.), (one act), 1966.

WHITNEY, Elvie. Center of Darkness, (unprod.), (one act), 1968.

WHITNEY, Elvie. Pornoff, (one act), 1969.

WHITNEY, Elvie. Up a Little Higher, (unprod.), 1968.

WILLIAMS, Ellwoodson. Voice of the Gene, 1969.

WILLIAMS, Margaret. The Irregular Verb to Love, 1963. New
York: Samuel French, 1962. PAL

WILLIAMS, Tennessee. Period of Adjustment, 1960. New York:
New Directions, 1960.

WILLIS, Harold. A Sound of Silence, 1965. In Best Plays
of 1964-1965, Guernsey, Otis L. Jr. PAL

WILSON, Langford. The Calico Cat and the Gingham Dog, 1969.
New York: Dramatists Play Service, 1969.

WILSON, Sandy. Valmouth, (musical), 1960.

WOLCOTT, Derek. Malcochon, (one act), 1969. NEC

WYMAN, Joel. The Day of the Lion, 1964.

YANKOWITZ, Susan. Slaughterhouse Play. In Yale/Theatre,
Vol. 2, No. 2, (Summer, 1969).

ALGER, Esther M. Greater Love Hath No Man. KT

ALGER, Esther M. Tag End. KT

ANDERSON, Harold L. Smell the Sweet Savor.

ANONYMOUS. The Heart of the Blue Ridge. Typescript. PAL

ARDREY, Robert. Skin Deep.

ARKULES, Albert, and Bertkover, Jacob. Kappola. KT

BAKER, Ruby B. Overcoming. KT

BAKER, Ruby B. Primitive Baptist. KT

BANCROFT, J.W. This Freedom. KT

BENNETT, Isadora. Coastwise. KT

BENNETT, Isadora. Come Christmas. KT

BENNETT, Isadora. Deep Dark. KT

BERTKOVER, Jacob, and Arkules, Albert. Kappola. KT

BOATNER, Edward. Jules Caesar in Rome, Georgia. Typescript. PAL

BONTEMPS, Arna. When the Jack Hollers. Manuscript. YL

BRANCH, William. Experiment in Black.

BRYANT, Hazel. Keys to the Kingdom. KT

BURRIS, Andrew. You Must Be Born Again. KT

BUTCHER, James W. Milk and Honey.

CESAIRE, Aime. King Christophe. NEC

CHAPMAN, Tedwell. Dusky Gods. KT

CHARASH, Jack. King Henry. FTP

CHASE, Richard. Home to Caanan. KT

CHILD, Nellise. People of the Cage, (one act). FTP

COOKSEY, Curtis. Starlight. KT

COURTNEY, Ward. Trilogy in Black. FTP

CULLEN, Countee. Byword For Evil (Medea). Manuscript. YL

DAVENPORT, Butler. The Father's Sons.

DAVIDSON, Gerald. Fresh Out of Heaven. KT

DAVIS, Ossie. A Last Dance for Sybil, (unprod.).

DAWSON, James, and Ligon, Helen. Cockboat Landing, (one act).

DISNEY, Loren. Land of Cotton. KT

DODSON, Owen. Americus. Manuscript. YL

DODSON, Owen. Black Mother Praying. Manuscript. YL

DODSON, Owen. Climbing to the Soul. YL

DODSON, Owen. Don't Give Up the Ship. Manuscript. YL

DODSON, Owen. Heroes on Parade No. 3: Climb to the Soul. Manuscript. YL

DODSON, Owen. Lord Nelson, Naval Hero. Manuscript. YL

DODSON, Owen. Jonathan's Song. Manuscript. YL

DODSON, Owen. Old Ironsides. Manuscript. YL

DOWNING, Henry F. The Exiles.

DOWNING, Henry F. Melic Ric.

DOWNING, Henry F. The Sinews of War.

DOWNING, Henry F. The Statue and the Wasp.

DOWNING, Henry F. Which Should She Have Saved.

DUNCAN, Isadore. Full Moonlight. KT

DUNCAN, Isadore. God's Own. KT

DUNCAN, Thelma. The Scarlet Shawl, (one act).

ENGLISH, H.C. King Christopher. KT

EVANS, J. Wellington. The Other Woman. KT

EYRE, Lawrence. Syrus Matarzus. KT

FITZGERALD, Russell. Sabus. Typescript. NEC

GILBERT, Mercedes. In Greener Pastures.

GILBERT, Ralph M. Judas Iscariot. Manuscript. YL

GOLDSMITH, Gloria. The Compensation Factor. Typescript.
    NEC

GRAHAM, Pearl. Clotfield.

GRAHAM, Shirley. Elijah's Ravens. KT

GRAHAM, Shirley. Coal Dust. KT

GRAHAM, Shirley. It's Morning. KT

GRAHAM, Shirley. Track 13. KT

GREENSFELDER, Elmer. Nobody Knows. KT

GRIFFITH, Rose. Corner on William. KT

HAMILTON, Harry Lacy. Paducah in Tuxedo. KT

HENNEKE, Ben Graf. Day Coach. KT

HENNEKE, Ben Graf. Good Old War. KT

HINKSON, Larry L. Beautiful Flowers, (musical).

HUGHES, Langston. Angelo Herndon Jones, (one act). Manuscript. YL

HUGHES, Langston. Drums of Haiti. Manuscript. YL

HUGHES, Langston. Outshines the Sun. YL

HUGHES, Langston. Trouble with the Angels. KT

HUGHES, Will. No Left Turn. KT

HUNTER, Paul. Where The Promised Land. Typescript. NEC

HURSTON, Zora. From Sun to Sun.

JACKSON, Nagle (director). America: Black and White. Typescript. PAL

JACOBI, Paula. The Adams. KT

JACOBI, Paula. Spare Rib.

JELLIFFE, Rowena, and Mulhauser, Roland. One Hundred in the Shade. KT

JOHNSON, Georgia Douglas. The Starting Point, (one act). Manuscript. YL

LEDERER, Clara. Osceola. KT

LEE, Frank. Smoke Dreams. KT

LESSER, Robert. The White King of the Black Canaries. Typescript. NEC

MCCLURE, Marjorie. Marriage of King Paulinus. KT

MCLEOD, Norman. Death Valley. KT

MARTIN, James M. Dixieland. Typescript. PAL

MARTIN, James M. A Kentucky Gentleman. Typescript. PAL

MATHEUS, John. Quanga, (opera).

MOORE, George A. Where There Are Two. KT

MULHAUSER, Roland A. Black Thunder. Manuscript. YL

MULHAUSER, Roland, and Jelliffe, Rowena. One Hundred
in the Shade. KT

OLNEER, Richard, and Tejas, Jonathan. Half Brothers.
Typescript. PAL

O'MALLEY, Martin J. Hammer Crump. Typescript. NEC

O'MALLEY, Martin J. Louis Marsh. Typescript. NEC

O'MALLEY, Martin J. Soul Brother's Hang-Up, (one act).
Typescript. NEC

O'MALLEY, Martin J. Tea For Three Billion, (one act).
Typescript. NEC

PALMER, Anne, and Smedley, Katharine. Hanging Out the
Wash, (one act). In Plays. Philadelphia: Penn Publishing
Co., n.d.

PAULL, Irene. A Million Black and White Are Saying No!
Typescript. PAL

PAXTON, Dorothy. River Town. KT

PERKINS, Chic. The Darktown Jubilee. Typescript. PAL

PRATT, Raymond. The Infection of Chrom. Typescript. NEC

REEVES, Theodore. Beggars Are Coming to Town. Typescript.
PAL

RICHARDSON, Thomas. Protest.

RICHARDSON, Willis. The Amateur Prostitute. Typescript. Schom

RICHARDSON, Willis. Bold Lover, (one act). Typescript.
Schom

RICHARDSON, Willis. The Brown Boy, (one act). Typescript. Schom

RICHARDSON, Willis. The Curse of the Shell Road Witch, (one
act). Typescript. Schom

RICHARDSON, Willis. The Dark Haven, (one act). Typescript.
Schom

RICHARDSON, Willis. A Ghost of the Past, (one act). In
Plays. Dayton, Ohio: Paine Publishing Co., (pamphlets).

RICHARDSON, Willis. Hope of the Lonely. KT

RICHARDSON, Willis. Imp of the Devil, (one act).
Typescript. Schom

RICHARDSON, Willis. The Jail Bird, (one act). Typescript.
Schom

RICHARDSON, Willis. Joy Rider. Typescript. Schom

RICHARDSON, Willis. The Man Who Married a Young Wife,
(one act). Typescript. Schom

RICHARDSON, Willis. The Nude Siren, (one act). Typescript.
Schom

RICHARDSON, Willis. A Pillar of the Church, (one act).
Typescript. Schom

RICHARDSON, Willis. Rooms for Rent, (one act). Typescript.
Schom

RICHARDSON, Willis. The Visiting Lady. Typescript. Schom

ROSS, John M. Dog's Place. KT

SAVAGE, George, and George Jr. The Garbage Hustlers. Typescript. PAL

SAVAGE, George, and George Jr. Leehomer, (one act),
(unprod.).

SAVAGE, George, and George Jr. The Year of the Sit-In,
(trilogy of one acts).

SCHOENFELD, Bernard. Trouble With The Angels, (one act).

SEILER, Conrad. Darker Brother. KT

SEILER, Conrad. End of the World. KT

SHAPPIN, Irwin. Black Belt, (one act).

SMEDLEY, Katharine, and Palmer, Anne. Hanging Out the Wash,
(one act). In Plays. Philadelphia: Penn Publishing Co.

SMITH, Caleb. A Dawn, A Morning's Work. Typescript. NEC

SMITH, Caleb. The Cocktail Hour. Typescript. NEC

SMITH, Caleb. A Daisy Chain, (one act). Typescript. NEC

SMITH, J.A. Just Ten Days. KT

ST AMBLER, Peter Land. The Deliverance. Typescript. NEC

STEPHENS, N. Bagby. Karamu. KT

SWANSON, Walter S.J. Nigerinde! The First Bad Sojourns of
Young Miss Truth, The New York Slave. Typescript. NEC

TEJAS, Jonathan, and Olneer, Richard. Half Brothers.
Typescript. PAL

TILLMAN, Katherine Davis. Aunt Betsy's Thanksgiving.
Philadelphia: A.M.E. Book Concern. Schom

TOWNS, George. Sharecropper.

TROUTMAN, Doris. The Falling of the Moon, (one act). FTP

VELASQUEZ, Juan. An Empty Wait. Typescript. NEC

WARD, Theodore. Falcon of Adowa. KT

WARD, Theodore. Sick and Tired. KT

WARD, Theodore. Whole Hog or Nothing.

WATKINS, Maurine. Marshland. KT

WILLIAMS, Eugene. Return of John Evans. KT

WILLIAMS, Vincent. After a Lynch - Free Harvest. Manuscript.
  YL

ZAVIDOWSKY, Bernard. The Uncommitted. Typescript. NEC

ZIMMERMAN, Jess. The Ides of March. Typescript. NEC

AFTERWORD

Suggested Areas for Further Research

From the problems encountered in assembling this bibliography, it appears that there is a need for more precise information in several areas of Black American theatre history: 1) the musicals and revues written by Blacks in the late 19th and early 20th century; 2) the non-professional productions by Black groups and community theatres; 3) the dramatic productions in Negro schools and colleges over the last 100 years.

For the musicals written by Black authors from the 1890's to World War I, the books and often even the music and lyrics are not extant. Because many authors and composers collaborated – perhaps contributing only one song to a production – it is difficult to credit authorship. To enter one show title under six or seven names seems excessive for a bibliography of this kind. Music historians either ignore these musicals or present conflicting information about who created what parts, when it was done, and where. Yet these musicals are the doors through which the American Blacks entered the commercial theatre; indeed, these musicals did much to create American musical theatre. To fail to credit these men and their work is tantamount to condoning the racist character of our past and present.

The problems of collaboration extends beyond the early musicals. For example, a major author, Mr. Langston Hughes, not only wrote a number of dramatic and poetical-dramatic scripts, but he collaborated often, made revisions, changed titles, sought new collaborators, returned to old projects, etc. At this writing, the manuscripts of Langston Hughes deposited in the James Weldon Johnson Memorial Collection at Yale University Library are not accessible. I have relied upon the assistance of the Curator, Mr. Arna Bontemps, to indicate which Hughes' dramatic scripts are deposited at Yale, and with whom Mr. Hughes collaborated.

In addition to the letters, diaries, journals, and news accounts in Negro newspapers and periodicals – which have yet to be sought out and written about – there are yet living a number of theatre men who worked in the early part of this century. I refer to men like Leigh Whipper, Avon Long, Noble Sissle, and Willis Richardson. Oral histories should be collected from these and many others. Mr. Vantile Whitfield of the Performing Arts Society of Los Angeles has told me that he is doing some of this important work.

The plays and productions of a number of Southern schools need to be recorded and explored. Men like Randolph Edmonds, Thomas Pawley, Thomas Poag, and John Ross have been writing and producing Black theatre for many years. We should no longer rely so heavily upon a few published sources like J.W. Johnson's Black Manhattan; the Black theatre is and has been more than New York City.

BIBLIOGRAPHY

In a bibliography of 2,000 entries the difficulty of finding and reading every play is formidable. I read several hundred plays, I glanced through many more, but finally I had to rely upon other bibliographers. This work relies heavily upon bibliographies in the following theses and dissertations:

Belcher, Fannin S., Jr. The Place of the Negro in the Evolution of the American Theatre, 1767-1940. Ph.D. Yale, 1945.

Blitgen, Sister Mary John Carol. Voices of Protest: An Analysis of the Negro Protest Plays of the 1963-1964 Broadway and Off-Broadway Season. M.A., University of Kansas, 1966.

Bond, Frederick W. The Direct and Indirect Contribution Which the American Negro Has Made to the Drama and the Legitimate Stage, With Underlying Conditions Responsible. Ph.D., New York, 1938.

Bradley, Gerald S., Jr. The Negro in the American Drama, 1893-1917. MFA, Carnegie Institute of Technology, 1963.

Cowan, Mary Frances. The Negro in the American Drama, 1877-1900. M.S., Howard University, 1950.

Eikleberry, Burton. The Negro Actor's Participation and the Negro Image on the New York Stage, 1954-1964. M.A., University of Kansas, 1965.

Kuhlke, William. They Too Sing America, The New Negro as Portrayed by Negro Playwrights, 1918-1930. M.A., University of Kansas, 1959.

Pettit, Paul Bruce. The Important American Dramatic Types to 1900, A Study of the Yankee, Negro, Indian, and Frontiersman. Ph.D., Cornell University, 1949.

Sherman, Alfonso. The Diversity of Treatment of the Negro Character in American Drama Prior to 1860. Ph.D., Indiana University, 1964.

Troesch, Helen De Rusha. The Negro in English Dramatic Literature and On the Stage. Ph.D., Western Reserve University, 1940.

In addition to theses and dissertations, the following books and bibliographies were most helpful.

Abramson, Doris. Negro Playwrights in the American Theatre, 1925–1959. New York: Columbia University Press, 1969.

Blesh, Rudi, and Janis, Harriet. They All Played Ragtime. New York: Alfred A. Knopf, 1950.

Brown, Sterling. The Negro Poetry and Drama. Washington, 1937. Reprinted New York: Atheneum, 1969.

Burton, Jack. The Blue Books of Broadway Musicals. Watkins Glen, N.Y.: Century House, 1952.

Federal Theatre Project. National Service Bureau Publications, New York: 1936.

Hughes, Langston, and Meltzer, Milton. Black Magic. Englewood Cliffs, New Jersey: Prentice-Hall, Inc., 1968.

Hutton, Laurence. Curiosities of the American Stage. New York: Harper Bros., 1891.

Isaacs, Edith J. The Negro in the American Theatre. New York: Theatre Arts, 1947.

Johnson, James Welden. Black Manhattan. New York: Knopf, 1930.

Lawson, Hilda J. Bibliography of Contemporary Negro Drama, Urbana, Illinois, 1939.

Locke, Alain. "Bibliography of Negro Drama" from Plays of Negro Life. New York: Harper Bros., 1927.

Mitchell, Loften. Black Drama: The Story of the American Negro in the Theatre. New York: Hawthorne Books, 1967.

Moody, Richard. America Takes the Stage. Bloomington, Ind.: 1955.

Moody, Richard. Dramas From the American Theatre, 1762-1909. New York: World Publishing Co., 1966.

Nagle, Father Urban. Behind the Masque. New York: Mullen Books, 1951.

Odell, George E.D. Annals of the New York Stage. 13 Vols. New York: 1927.

Patterson, Lindsay (comp.). Anthology of the American Negro in the Theatre. New York: The Publishers Co., 1967.

Quinn, Arthur H. A History of the American Drama. New York: F.S. Crofts and Co., 1936.

Ralph, George. The American Theater, The Negro and the Freedom Movement. Hope College, 1964 (mimeograph).

Reardon, William, and Pawley, Thomas. Bibliography on Black Theatre and Drama. University of Santa Barbara, 1969 (mimeograph).

Among the periodicals, Crisis, Opportunity, and Phylon were found useful.

The following Black authors submitted their bibliographies by letter: Randolph Edmonds; Ted Shine; Loften Mitchell; Abram Hill; William Branch; Lonne Elder III; Arna Bontemps; Owen Dodson; LeRoi Jones; John Ross; Laura Ann Miller; Otis Greene; Jack Romaner Strong; Vantile Whitfield; Evan Walker; Thurman W. Stanback; Thomas Pawley; Charles Fuller; Ossie Davis; Val Ferdinand; Ellwoodson Williams; Willis Richardson; Tom Harris. The New Lafayette Theatre Agency sent bibliographies on Ed Bullins; Ben Caldwell; Marvin X; and Salimu.

TITLE INDEX

130

135

139

145

AUTHOR INDEX

ADDENDA

BARSHA, Tony. Nigger Nate, (one act), 1970.

BASS, George H. Black Blues, 1968.

BASS, George H. The Fun House, 1968.

BASS, George H. The How Long Sweet, 1969.

BASS, George H. The Third Party, 1968.

BASS, George H. A Trio for the Living, 1968.

CHILDRESS, Alice. Wine in the Wilderness, 1969. New York: Dramatists Play Service, 1969.

DAVIS, Milburn. Nightmare, (unprod.), 1970.

FELTON, Haleemon. Backstage.

FELTON, Haleemon. Drifting Souls.

FELTON, Haleemon. House of Eternal Darkness.

GILBERT, Mercedes. Ma Johnson's Harlem Rooming House (serial), 1938.

HUGHES, Langston. The Em-Furher Jones, (one act), 1938. Manuscript. YL

HUGHES, Langston. Emperor of Haiti, 1936(?). Typescript, 1963. Schom

HUGHES, Langston. Front Porch, 1934(?). Microfilm, 1962. Schom

HUGHES, Langston, and Hurston, Zora. Mule Bone, (act III only). In Drama Critique, (The Negro in the Theatre), (Spring 1964). Schom

HUGHES, Langston. The Organizer, (one act), (unprod.). 1938/9. Manuscript. YL

HUGHES, Langston, and Still, William Grant. Troubled Island, 1949, (an opera version of Emperor of Haiti). New York: Leeds Music Corporation, 1949. PAL

HURSTON, Zora, and Hughes, Langston. Mule Bone, (act III only). In Drama Critique, (The Negro in the Theatre), (Spring 1964). Schom

KENNEDY, Adrienne. The Son, (one act), 1970.

LEVIN, Herman, and Smith, Oliver. Bless You All, (revue), 1950.

LINDSAY, Powell. Young Man of Harlem, (unprod.), 1938.

MACKEY, William. Billy No Name, (musical), 1970.

MASON, Clifford. Sister Sadie, (unprod.), 1970.

REID, Ira De A. John Henry.

ROSS, John. Half Caste Moon.

ROSS, John. The Purple Lily.

SMITH, Oliver, and Levin, Herman. Bless You All, (revue), 1950.

STILL, William Grant, and Hughes, Langston. Troubled Island, 1949,
    (an opera version of Emperor of Haiti). New York: Leeds Music
    Corporation, 1949. PAL

TOLSON, Melvin. Black Boy.

TOLSON, Melvin. The Fire in the Flint.

TOLSON, Melvin. The Moses of Beale Street.

TOLSON, Melvin. Southern Front.

VANE, Thaddeus. The Alligators are Coming, 1970.

WARD, Theodore. John Brown, 1950. In Masses and
    Mainstream (Act I, Sc. 4 only), Vol. 2,
    No. 10, (Oct. 1949). NYP

WALTON, Lester, and Troy, Henry. Darkeydom,
    (musical), 1914.

WILLIAMS, Ellwoodson. Mine Eyes Have Seen the Glory,
    (unprod.), 1970.

WILSON, Frank. Back Home Again, (one act).

WILSON, Frank. The Frisco Kid, (one act).

WILSON, Frank. The Good Sister Jones, (one act).